TAMING the BEAR

CHRISTOPHER TATE

Wrightbooks

Wrightbooks Pty Ltd
PO Box 270
Elsternwick
Victoria 3185

Ph: (03) 9532 7082
Fax: (03) 9532 7084
Email: wbooks@ozemail.com.au
Web site: www.wrightbooks.com.au

National Library of Australia cataloguing-in-publication data:

Tate, Christopher
Taming the bear: the art of trading a choppy market

1. Stock exchanges. 2. Stocks. 3. Investment analysis. 4. Portfolio management
I. Title

Includes index.
ISBN 1 875857 80 X.

332.642

Cover design by Rob Cowpe

The cover image was obtained from IMSI's MasterClips/MasterPhotos© Collection
1895 Francisco Blvd. East, San Rafael, CA 94901-5506, USA

The charts in this book were created using SuperCharts

Printed in Australia by Australian Print Group
ISBN: 1 875857 80 X

CONTENTS

PREFACE

IF ASKED TO define a bear market, most investors would say that it is a period of continually declining prices in the entire market. Such an answer would be only partly correct. A bear market may encompass the entire market, but it can also affect a subsection of the market, such as gold stocks (as in 1997), or an individual stock, such as BHP.

Furthermore, a bear market may not actually entail prices falling; prices may just drift sideways in a narrow band for a period of time.

Our definition of a bear market, therefore, is any period when prices are not trending up. This period may be a week, a month or several years. To some extent we are not concerned with time, merely the opportunity to profit from a recognisable period of either price decline or consolidation.

It is important for market participants to realise that the markets are not merely an elevator that goes one way, although this is a view held by many investment advisers, journalists and various "gurus". Prices spend as much time going down as they do going up, and they spend the bulk of their time drifting in broad consolidation patterns. In fact, it has been estimated that the prices in all markets – be it shares, commodities or currencies – spend as much as 80% of their time going sideways. Traditionally, such a situation would be extremely frustrating for average market participants, since they would, through a lack of knowledge, be unable to recognise that prices are going sideways. And if they did recognise this, they would lack the techniques to trade and profit from these sideways moves.

> **"All men can see those tactics whereby I conquer, but what none can see is the strategy out of which victory is evolved."**
>
> *SUN TZU, THE ART OF WAR, 6TH CENTURY B.C.*

This book hopes to address both of these problems by demonstrating how to recognise bear markets as they emerge and how to trade both the sudden whips down and the broader consolidation patterns that they can represent. If you only have the intellectual or emotional capacity to trade bull markets, you are missing out on a whole range of opportunities offered by the market, and it will be a long time between drinks for you.

Christopher Tate
Melbourne,
January, 1999

PART I

BEAR SPOTTING

> **"In individuals, insanity is rare, but in groups, parties, nations and epochs it is the rule."**
>
> *NIETZSCHE*

1: THE PSYCHOLOGY OF BEAR MARKETS

BEFORE BEGINNING AN exploration of the various techniques and methodologies of bear market identification and trading, it is necessary to understand something about the psychology of the market. This chapter will set the tone for the rest of the book in that it will attempt to distil many of the motivations of traders during market swings.

It has always been my contention that trading is primarily a psychological endeavour, and as such we need to understand our fellow traders. Once we understand what drives others to make decisions, our understanding of market dynamics is greatly enhanced. We will know why volume spikes at either the top or bottom of ranges, and how we can use this as a trading tool. We will know when to anticipate a change in market sentiment and how far this potential change is likely to go.

THE BULL/BEAR MARKET CYCLE

The bull/bear market cycle is the broadest definition we can possibly have regarding the cyclical nature of the market. Put simply, the market is initially dominated by the bulls. This is followed by an uneasy interregnum, followed by a swing in sentiment towards the bears. It is obvious that at any one point there will be a successful group, whose market view is confirmed by the current market trend, and an unsuccessful group, whose view is contrary to the trend.

Each of these groups will have differing characteristics. The successful traders will be motivated largely by greed, and will tend to congregate in groups with other like-minded traders. This grouping together reinforces the prevailing opinion of the herd, thereby further driving prices in a given direction and further enhancing the success of the group. This is largely why trends, when started, continue: they exist on a limited-feedback loop that is reinforced for an indefinite period of time. If you want a practical example of this, take time to visit the market display area outside one of the exchanges. During bull markets, you will notice very large congregations of amateur traders – in effect a small, rather directionless herd. Take time to watch the reaction of the crowd. The mood is generally buoyant, everyone is talkative, and positive opinions about the market are reinforced.

The unsuccessful group – whose opinions and strategies run counter to the prevailing market direction – has a different set of characteristics. Each member of the group is isolated and fearful. The members of the unsuccessful group are somewhat fragmented and disassociated from others. Again this can be seen in the market display area. Generally those by themselves during periods of peak market activity are those with a differing view to the majority. They may be long when it is time to be short, or vice versa. They might be attempting to counter-trend trade. This disassociation from the main group is to be expected. Within crowds, contrary opinions are not tolerated, and only become accepted when the opinion of the crowd changes. Consider the scene outside exchanges when market sentiment swings bearish very quickly. The majority of market participants never consider this to be a possibility. As such, their mood is pensive and withdrawn. There is no celebration, as everyone feels isolated within their own cocoon of fear.

"Within any market cycle, there will be those who are successful and those who are unsuccessful."

Within any market cycle, there will be those who are successful and those who are unsuccessful. There is no discrimination as to whether you are successful during a bull or a bear market. The characteristics of each group remain the same. The successful move as a group, reinforcing prevailing opinions, and the unsuccessful are isolated and withdrawn.

This leads me to recommend some homework for traders. Spend a few days in the market display area of the stock exchange, observing people and how they react to changes in the market. Watch their facial expressions, their mood and the general level of noise. Such an experience will give you an insight into the psychology of crowds. Consider this little exercise to be the first step in understanding a subject I call "Trader's Anthropology 101". If you can gain insights into crowd behaviour, the indicators we will look at later will have more meaning, and they will provide you with a much greater intuitive sense of what is happening in the market.

REASONS FOR PRICE REVERSAL

Trading is about spotting trends as they develop. Trends naturally arise out of price reversals, but the question is: why do prices reverse and new trends become established? The traditional answer to this question is that there is a change in underlying fundamentals, and this change is transmitted into the price. This argument is inherently flawed, since fundamentals often have no impact on price whatsoever, and whatever influence they do have is filtered and distilled by the perceptions of the traders who make up the market.

There is a simpler, more efficient answer as to why trends persist and then change. A trend will continue in a given direction for as long as there are new market participants to give it impetus. Quite simply, a trend will continue as long as there is new money. This is why reversals come at extremes of sentiment. Markets become bullish when everyone is bearish, and vice versa. As an example, consider the following chart.

FIG. 1.1 – MARKET REVERSALS

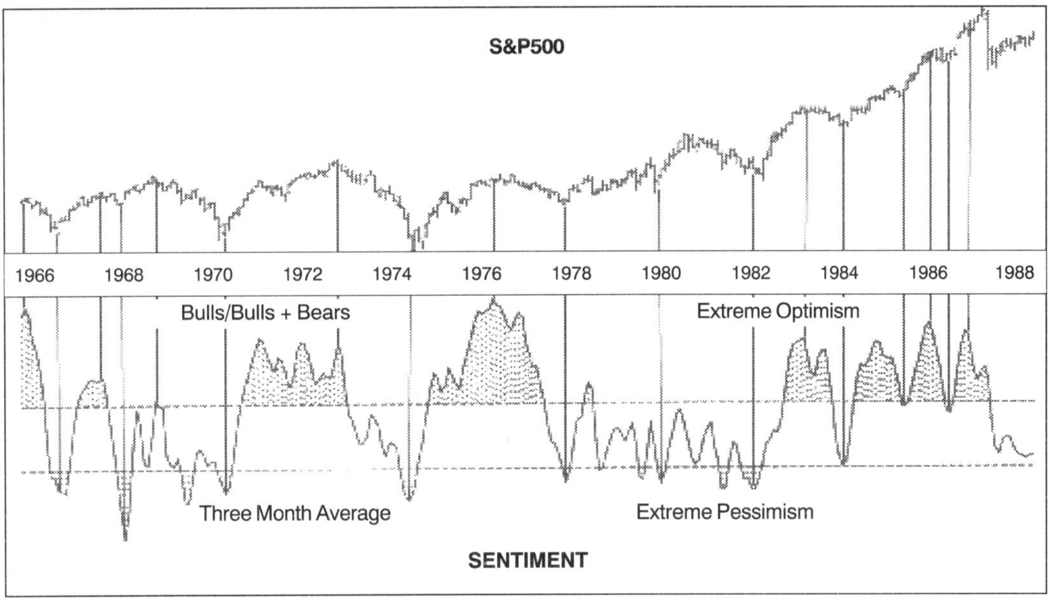

One point is immediately apparent – market reversals occur as sentiment peaks in either a bullish or bearish direction. In the case of swings from bull to bear markets, the market becomes bearish when everyone is bullish. If you consider this, it is extremely logical. Investor expectations are simply irrational in respect to the potential gains left in a given move. As such, these expectations are easily deflated and are prone to wild swings. Such a development is quite easy for the average market participant to imagine. Consider the last time you had a trade that was profitable. It is most likely that your mood was positive and optimistic. You probably assumed that the move would go on forever. Now contrast this mood with how you felt when this trade started to go bad. Your mood probably swung from wildly positive to the depths of despair. Trading can be an extremely emotional endeavour, and many treat a reversal of fortune as if the love of their life had just left them. This is the behaviour of crowds, and it is replicated in each individual who makes up the crowd.

If you think such behaviour is only the preserve of the amateur trader, consider the following table (Table 1.1).

TABLE 1.1 – "FORECASTING" RECORD OF MUTUAL FUNDS BASED ON CASH-TO-ASSETS RATIO

DATE		FUNDS "PREDICTION"		FUNDS "PREDICTION"	
MONTH	YEAR	BULLISH	BEARISH	RIGHT	WRONG
July	1956	*			✖
June	1958		*		✖
April	1959	*			✖
September	1960		*		✖
December	1961	*			✖
September	1962		*		✖
November	1964	*			✖
October	1966		*		✖
September	1967	*		✔	
March	1968		*		✖
December	1968	*			✖
July	1970		*		✖
April	1972	*			✖
September	1974		*		✖
September	1976	*			✖
March	1978		*		✖
September	1978	*		✔	
May	1980		*		✖
March	1981	*			✖
June	1982		*		✖
December	1983	*			✖
June	1984		*		✖
March	1985	*		✔	
October	1985		*		✖
February	1986	*		✔	
September	1986		*		✖
March	1987	*			✖
April	1988		*		✖

This table tracks the performance of mutual funds in the United States for the period 1956 to 1988. It analyses the cash-to-assets ratio of the funds, and then uses this as an indicator of whether the fund is bullish or bearish. This investment stance is then reviewed to see if the funds' predictions were correct.

In a sample period of 32 years, the fund managers got it right on only four occasions, and these four instances can be put down to coincidence. What was found was the funds were most bearish, i.e. fully invested in cash, as the market became bullish, and they were most bullish, i.e. fully invested in equities, before markets peaked. These funds displayed exactly the same irrational behaviour as the majority of market participants. There is no reason to believe that these particular observations regarding fund managers do not apply in Australia.

In returning to the reasons why trends change, there is an even simpler explanation than the psychological characteristics of traders. Trends simply run out of steam when there are not enough new market entrants to sustain a move. Prices reverse when the investment community is fully committed to a given point of view.

This can be illustrated with an analogy. Imagine there is a group of people pushing a car up a gradually-steepening hill. Each time the gradient increases, a new member is added to the team at the back of the car. This would not be a problem if the gradient was increasing at the same rate with which fresh pushers were arriving. Imagine, though, that the gradient is increasing at a rate greater than that with which fresh pushers are arriving. Sooner or later, simple physics wins. The team are no longer able to maintain forward momentum. Their efforts stall, and the car begins to move backwards, despite frantic efforts to move it ahead. These last-ditch efforts can be seen in the terminal phases of price moves, as traders attempt to push prices higher. Such activity shows up as volume spikes, and is referred to as "climax" or "blow off" volume. I prefer to think of it as the bulls going under for the final time.

THE REVERSAL PROCESS

What we have examined so far has provided a broad overview of the behaviour of crowds when markets pivot through their broadest of cycles. The next step is to apply this to a real-world example and to see what sort of insights this understanding can bring us. More importantly, we want to see how this knowledge can help us to be more profitable in our trading.

The chart on the following page (Fig. 1.2) is of BHP, and was chosen because of the sustained bear market BHP endured after attempting to move to a new high. As such, it is ideal for examining the reversal process and how this process influenced traders to change their opinions. This, in turn, changed prices and the prevailing trend.

Three points are noted on the chart: the reversal point, the retest and the confirmation of the new trend.

FIG. 1.2 – BHP REVERSAL PROCESS (1997)

The Reversal Point

At the reversal point, the majority of traders involved in BHP held the same opinion. This opinion roughly went along these lines: good shares always make new highs, my broker says it's going to reach $30, we are in the middle of a bull market, good shares never go down, etc., etc. Each one of these phrases is designed to confirm the prevailing opinion, and imagery such as saying a share is cheap or undervalued is very powerful. Crowds are susceptible to very simple phrases, since, as we have seen, the market is a very emotional place, and reason dissipates in the face of positive emotions. These powerful phrases also have the added weight of being elucidated by someone in a perceived position of authority: a broker. As such, many in the market take these pronouncements to be some sort of mysterious divinity that should not be questioned. The power of the expert should not be underestimated in shaping the beliefs of the investing public. These beliefs are also reinforced by the fear of missing out on future gains.

However, as we have seen, there is simply not enough money to sustain continual moves in a given direction, and momentum will falter. This faltering can be seen in the first part of the move away from the high. It is important to note that this initial move down is the reversal point. The underlying sentiment in the market is beginning to change.

Some astute traders will have seen this change in tone and will begin to sell. Prices are now in an uneasy equilibrium between bullish and bearish. This unease is beginning to filter into the mood of market participants, since prices are beginning to slip against positive expectations. The successful group – who have ridden BHP up – are now in danger. Despite this, they will cling to their positive expectations, even in the face of mounting evidence against them.

The Retest

This phase is the last attempt by the bulls, who had been very successful, to reassert themselves, and momentarily their beliefs are confirmed, as the stock rallies. Their fear of missing out on potential gains is somewhat assuaged. This is a classic bear trap, and it constantly catches the unwary. It is at this point that technical indicators will contradict the move up. Astute traders with a good trading method will now be getting extremely powerful sell signals. Sentiment has swung the way of the bear. The bears are about to become the successful group, and the bulls are about to feel the pain of unrealised expectations. Fear starts to raise its head among the bulls, as expectations diverge from reality. Traders have gone from expectations of a never-ending series of highs to the unpalatable truth that prices may actually decline. The interesting point to note is that this fear does not translate into action, as we will see in a later chart. Fear among market participants is initially manifested as paralysis, as they face mounting evidence that their opinion is wrong.

"This is a classic bear trap, and it constantly catches the unwary."

The Confirmation of the New Trend

Crowd sentiment changes at this point. The downward spikes in price shake more of the bulls from their positions, and they join the bears. The crowd now starts to look for justification of its opinion in the underlying fundamentals of price. Note that price comes before fundamentals. Fundamentals serve merely to reinforce existing feelings about a move.

In the case of BHP, it was easy to find fundamentals to justify the decision to be short. Commodity prices were poor, senior management seemed incapable of running a hot bath, BHP was being squeezed in all its markets, the Asian economic crisis meant a general downturn in business. Yet these factors took hold in the minds of traders only after prices began to slip, and in the minds of some in the market-place these factors held no sway at all, and they continued to buy on the way down.

Those who bought all the way down are eternal bulls, and are myopically optimistic and generally lacking a sense of reality. It should also be noted that there are eternal bears, who are consistently negative in their trading stance. Neither group is successful.

WHAT HAPPENS IN THE MINDS OF TRADERS

The following chart of BHP provides a look at some of the thoughts and emotions that go through the minds of the average participants as they are faced with the vagaries of the market.

FIG. 1.3 – TRADER PSYCHOLOGY

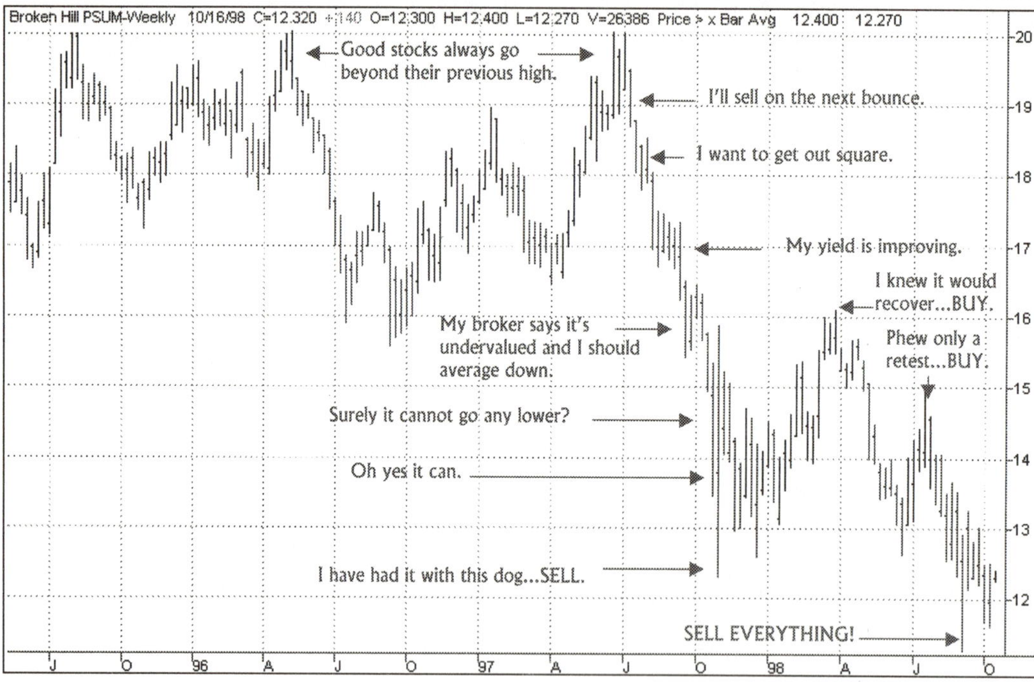

This somewhat facetious look at trader psychology translates many of the more esoteric concepts we have looked at so far into the true thoughts and emotions of the average trader. Most traders will recognise some of these sentiments.

It is possible to see these concepts in the way the ordinary trader behaves. Market tops are accompanied by a belief that the good times won't end. This is precisely the time when markets change their tone. Then we see an inability by traders to act when confronted by reality, and a dislocation between expectations and reality. The expert – in this case the broker – attempts to allay fears, and consequently steers traders into a greater loss. Disbelief that prices could actually go any lower – and the crushing realisation that they can go lower – is followed by the inevitable sale at the bottom of the cycle.

"People don't want to learn how to trade. They want to be told what to do."

FLOOR SAYING

This pattern then reverses itself on the way up. Traders buy at the next immediate peak. Once again they are comforted by the belief that shares always go up, or that it was $20, it is now $15, surely it is better value. (This is my favourite argument, because its logical end point is that shares are at their best when they have zero value.) There is some relief as prices retest their low, followed by the heartbreak of a ruined romance and the eventual complete withdrawal from the market. This is why traders' disassociation from the market is so extreme when confronted by losses. Their confidence has been shattered. The illusions they held regarding their competency are ruined. Nobody likes to confront failure, and only very successful traders do confront their own failings. The majority simply slide away, hurt and disappointed, their love affair with the market in tatters.

This brings me to a final point. During bull markets, many traders see the market as a hobby. Teenagers collect CDs or play sport, and there comes a time when these hobbies are no longer of interest. The CDs collect dust and the footy boots sit in the garage. The bulk of bull market traders are no different. They stay whilst the going is easy, and disappear when the going gets a little more challenging. If this is you, then this book is not for you – following are practical mechanisms for dealing with choppy markets.

You will not find the Holy Grail in these pages. I make you no promises at all. Trading is a psychological endeavour, which is why I began this journey with an introductory look at trader psychology. Your success or failure will come down to how you deal with your own psychology during trading. I can only give you the tools – neither I nor anybody else can force you to use them in a manner that works for you.

2: HOW TO IDENTIFY A BEAR MARKET

IF YOU HAVE started your trading career during a bull market you are probably of the mindset that markets never go down. Unfortunately for you, this view is reinforced by a variety of semi-professional advisers, who are asking you to believe that the law of gravity has been repealed. Look carefully at this long-term chart of the All Ordinaries Index, and ask yourself what has changed so fundamentally that prices can never again endure a sustained downward turn.

FIG. 2.1 – ALL ORDINARIES MONTHLY

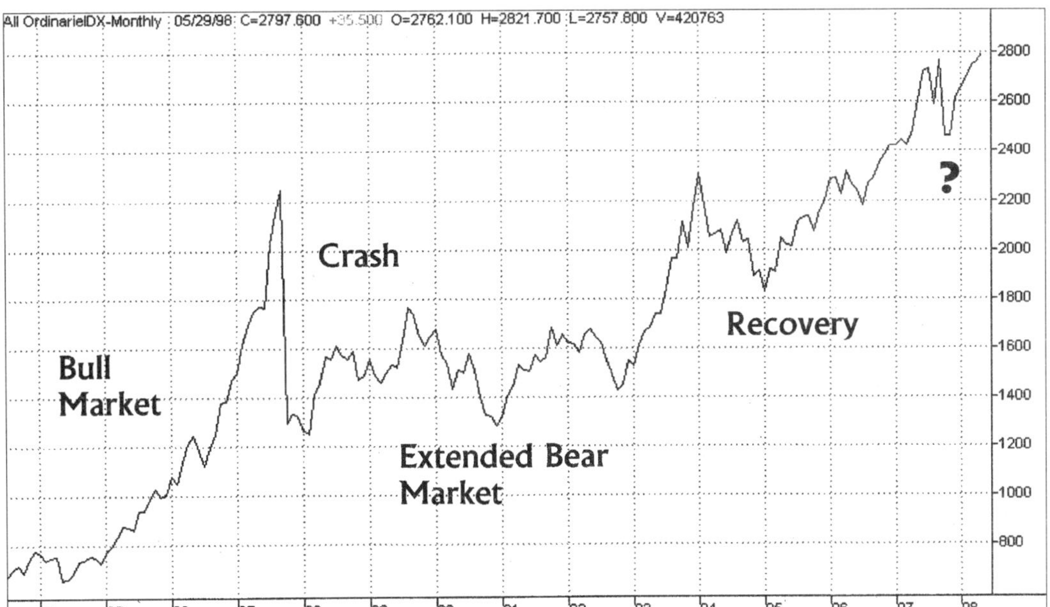

What is clear is that prices move in cycles, and these cycles can be clearly defined. The period from mid-1984 to October 1987 represented a bull market. A clear shattering of investor confidence occurred in October 1987 and an extended six-year bear market began, during which time the market traded in a range of about 400 points. The failure of the market, in early 1993, to break the lows of late 1989 and 1991 signalled the beginning of a rise in prices up to early 1994, when prices began a downward spike that lasted until mid-1995, when the market consolidated. A breach of this consolidation zone launched a bull market.

"Each cycle in the market has a variety of smaller cycles within it..."

However, the situation is a little more complex than merely dividing the market into uptrends, downtrends and periods of consolidation. You will notice the earlier definition of a bear market did not specify time: our definition of a bear market is independent of time. Each cycle in the market has a variety of smaller cycles within it, and each of these smaller cycles represents an opportunity to traders.

FIG. 2.2 – TRENDS IN THE ALL ORDINARIES

This chart shows that, within the prime band of consolidation – as defined by the rectangle covering the period 1988 to 1993 – there are a variety of stages in the market, so we have to be careful how we define broad market activity. To enhance our definition of a bear market, we have to narrow our focus and introduce an additional stage in market development. This introduction of another phase is necessary because, if we merely looked at the above chart, we would say that markets went straight from bull to bear, with the occasional zone of consolidation. This is, in fact, a false picture, and is due to the lack of definition that comes about because of the time scale of the chart. Monthly charts, as you would expect, lack the discrimination of charts that have a more narrow focus. It is therefore necessary to reduce our time scale to a more narrow range. Consider the following chart.

FIG. 2.3 – ALL ORDINARIES DAILY (1997-98)

This is a daily chart of the All Ordinaries Index for the latter part of 1997 and the early part of 1998. Again, it is easy to see the changes in market tone. The October 1997 shake-out came as the market exited a zone of consolidation. It is interesting to note that the market talked itself into both the consolidation zone and the subsequent fall. For those of you who are interested in trader psychology – and that should be all of you – the fall in October 1997 came about because traders had talked themselves into believing that the tenth anniversary of the 1987 crash held some sort of mystical significance. Most traders believed that the market was overvalued and due for some form of shake-out: the Asian crisis merely provided the trigger. If it had not been the economic difficulties in Asia, another event would have shaken the market.

The market recovered quickly from the fall because everybody had wanted it to fall. In trading, the majority is always wrong. If people in the industry tell you to go long, then chances are that you will make more money going short, and vice versa. It is a perverse fact that when the herd is in agreement, it is generally wrong. As a consequence of this, the market recovered from the shock and continued to head back up.

> *TRADING RULE*
> **The herd is always wrong.** If the herd is calling for a fall in the midst of a strong uptrend, any move down will be short lived. If the herd is calling for a rally in a declining market then the rally will be short lived. Market reversals only occur when the herd believes that the market will never go down again. Conversely, lifts out of bear markets will only occur when the herd believes that prices will never go up again. As P. T. Barnum once said: *every crowd has a silver lining.*

However, even though we have reduced the discrimination of our chart, it still presents us with a slightly distorted view.

MARKET PHASES

There are four broad phases in market evolution:

- *Phase One* is a broad pattern of consolidation. This is traditionally the base or range from which prices break out.
- *Phase Two* is the uptrend formed by a break-out in prices.
- *Phase Three* is when prices consolidate as the last of the bulls enter the market. There is heavy resistance to prices moving any higher as bulls start to take profits and actively compete with the bears for the diminishing supply of buyers.
- *Phase Four* is when prices collapse as bears drive prices down. The last of the bulls are shaken out of their positions and panic sell, which often results in volume spikes.

These phases are shown in Fig. 2.4.

FIG. 2.4 – MARKET PHASES

MARKET VOLUME

Our identification of broad market cycles is incomplete without an ability to analyse volume and to understand its implications. Too many traders live by the old myth that you get paid on price, not volume. You don't get paid at all if you don't understand the mechanics of volume as they relate to changes in the market cycle.

In the consolidation phases, volume remains flat – like price, it trades in a range as market participants settle down. Neither bulls nor bears are in ascendancy during the consolidation phase. Prices are in equilibrium. As the base continues to form, volume may pick up marginally without having an adverse impact upon price. This is a very important development because it indicates that the stale bears no longer have sufficient energy to move prices lower. There are sufficient buyers to soak up stock at prevailing prices. The bulls who are returning to the market are not demanding any discount in price as compensation for picking up the stock. This is an important signal for the bear to be careful: the market is gaining strength, ever so subtly, and is preparing to break out. (As an aside, this is often a point at which the bulls get stuck in a range-trading market. Like bears, bulls are anxious to catch the next wave from the very beginning and they get in too soon.)

As the energy within the consolidation phase begins to build, so too does the volume. If you are short at this stage, watch out: the market has you in its sights. To simplify the identification of break-outs, a 21-day weighted moving average has been run through the price on Fig. 2.5. A break-out in this instance is signified by prices leaping above the moving average as volume accelerates. If you are a bear here you are facing the wrong direction and you are going to miss out on the opportunities presented by a rising market.

FIG. 2.5 – MARKET PHASES AND VOLUME

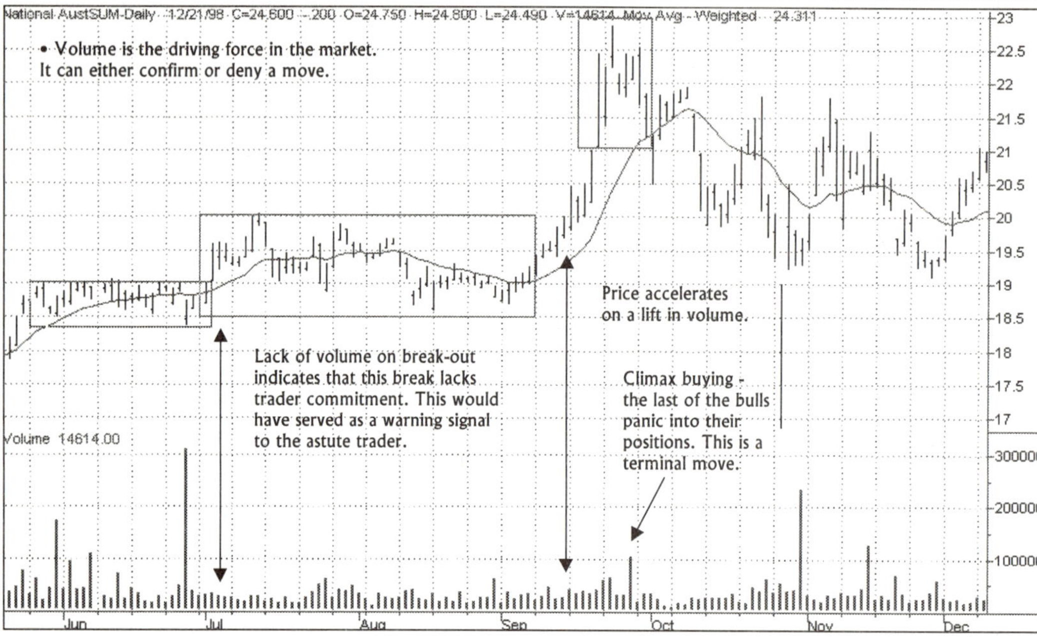

TRADING RULE

Never short a rising market. Sounds obvious, doesn't it? In fact, it is so obvious that traders do it nonetheless, often fuelling the bull market they are attempting to short.

Eventually prices begin to slow. As prices start to consolidate you may get severe spikes in volume. These represent panic-buying by the last of the bulls, who are anxious to jump on board. It is during this phase that bulls often believe prices cannot possibly go down, so they are willing to try and squeeze a little extra profit out of the market. It is at this point that prices begin to sag – the panic-buying by bulls is insufficient to maintain the market's momentum and prices consolidate. The market then begins to trade in a range.

This range-trading presents a specialised opportunity for the bear (techniques for dealing with this sort of market will be examined later). During this phase, prices are choppy and volume may, on average, be higher than during the phase one consolidation. The last of the bulls, unconvinced that prices have stalled, try to move the market higher, only to be met by equally aggressive bears. This is the time during which the bear is primed.

Just as prices broke out of phase one under volume, the same situation occurs with the drop out of the phase three consolidation. This is an important opportunity for the bear, and is the phase during which the greatest profits can be made.

Our definition of phases or market cycles helps us identify the broad patterns in the market, however it is still too broad an approach on which to base aggressive trading decisions. Despite this, understanding these basic cycles will help you, whether you are a portfolio trader who wants to know when to enter and exit the market or whether your trading focus is much narrower and involves the use of derivatives such as options, warrants or futures.

To actively trade the short side of the market, we need to hone our analysis so that we can make quality judgements about the health of the market and not be blind-sided by developments that we considered to be unexpected.

TRADING RULE

There are very few unexpected market developments. If it is unexpected to us then it merely means we did not consider all the possibilities. As a trader, expect the unexpected.

LOOK BEYOND THE MAJOR INDICES

When looking at bear markets, traders often fail to look beyond the major indices. The fairly myopic view is that if the All Ordinaries is going up then all stocks must be going up. Fortunately for those of us who like to trade the short side of markets, this is not the case. Markets are composed of a variety of elements, and each of these elements operates in its own cyclical manner.

Consider the two following charts: the first is BHP (Fig. 2.6), the second the All Ordinaries Index (Fig. 2.7). Notice how, as the All Ordinaries went through the normal phases of price activity – rises, declines, and some areas of consolidation – BHP entered a prolonged downturn, or bear phase, during which it lost almost 25% of its value.

Consider the chart of MIM (Fig. 2.8) for the period September 1997 to April 1998. From October, MIM endured a sustained downtrend. Compare its decline to the rises in the All Ordinaries Index (Fig. 2.9). We have a situation where the stocks that make up a particular index are showing their own patterns of price action that may be vastly different from those shown by the index.

FIG. 2.6 – BHP DAILY (1997)

FIG. 2.7 – ALL ORDINARIES DAILY (1997)

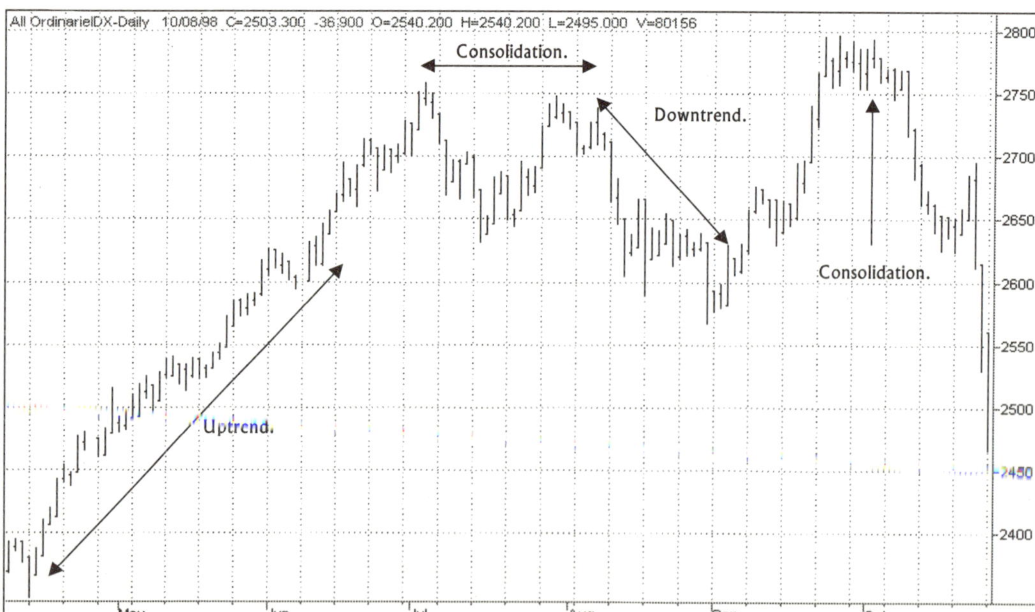

FIG. 2.8 – MIM HOLDINGS DAILY (1997-98)

FIG. 2.9 – ALL ORDINARIES DAILY (1997-98)

This variability in price action across markets will be a central theme throughout this book. Markets are not homogenous in their activity, and various trading opportunities occur at various times. The successful trader knows how to recognise and take advantage of all aspects of market behaviour. Traders will also need to know under what circumstances they should exit the market completely.

3: CAN WE PREDICT CRASHES?

THE ANSWER TO this question is *no*. There are a variety of individuals in the investment community who claim to have a psychic ability to predict the future. Unfortunately, they are long on hype and very short on facts. Many operate on the Chicken Little principle of running around yelling the sky is falling – if you keep saying it for long enough then sooner or later you are going to be correct.

"...you won't get anywhere at all if you are not facing the right direction."

This does not mean, however, that we cannot make reasoned judgements as to when markets may become intrinsically unstable or when a trend may change. It is the aim of this chapter to help you build a checklist of factors to look for in markets after they have undergone extended runs. Remember, we are only interested in catching changes in trends. We are not interested, by and large, in the magnitude of the trend or its duration – we only want to be facing in the right direction when the change occurs. Think of preparing for bear markets as a little like surfing: some waves will take you all the way to the shore, some will only take you part of the way and a small number will drop you on your head – but you won't get anywhere at all if you are not facing the right direction.

To form a checklist of indicators for determining when markets may become unstable at a fairly fundamental level, we need to take a look back at the last serious crash encountered by the market. The last serious shake-out in the market was in October 1987, and this collapse led to an extended bear market in which prices moved in a narrow range. However, it is important to realise that you cannot be myopic in your approach to trading: if the market is going up, take advantage of that and ride the bull run. Do not fall into the trap that many traders do of automatically assuming that, just because the market has gone up for a year, it is time for a crash or correction. As we have seen in the mid-1990s, markets can run for many years, and if you are a myopic bear then you will miss out on all those profit opportunities that accompany a rising market.

A HISTORY LESSON

In this section, we will draw on some of the material we have covered so far to get a cohesive picture of the market. To do this, we will look at the 1987 stock market crash.

FIG. 3.1 – DOW JONES INDEX (1987)

In 1987, the US market had been running up for almost four years. In mid-1987, the market slowed and prices consolidated, moving in a 200-point range for three-and-a-half months. This range-trading formed the basis for a phase one consolidation (see Fig. 3.1). In mid-June prices began to pick up speed again, and an explosive uptrend lifted the Dow 20% in eight weeks. Prices then slowed again and started to fatigue, drifting backwards and establishing a small downtrend. Prices, once again, started to recover and move back towards the old high as stale bears climbed on board, not wanting to miss out on the fun.

From this analysis in the last week of September 1987, we could have concluded that the market was moving higher. However, merely dividing the market into phases lacks sufficient incisiveness for us to make trading decisions. Once again we need to hone our analysis with further trend and sentiment-based tools. It is at this point in time that we need to take a step backwards and look at the bigger picture. All this analysis is taking place against the backdrop of historically high Price-to-Earnings ratios (see page 48 for an explanation of P/Es). We know from this that the market is at a level that is psychologically unstable, so in the back of our minds we know there is growing potential for a sudden sharp break in trader psychology. However, we also need to be aware that we have to be governed by our trading system. This is what we would do if we were in the market at this time.

If we move forward (Fig. 3.2), we see that our expected lift out of the downtrend has not occurred – in fact, prices have dropped sharply through our primary trend indicator: a 13-day moving average. In addition to this, the volume in the market is starting to lift on the downside – as astute bear market traders, we would now be facing in the short direction of the market. Our tools have flashed two warning lights: a sudden break in trend and a lift in volume. Note we are not expecting a crash – we cannot make that judgement – we are merely looking to take advantage of any weakness in the market. If the weakness is not confirmed we will simply alter our outlook so as to be able to trade the long side of the market.

FIG. 3.2 – DOW JONES INDEX WITH VOLUME INDICATOR

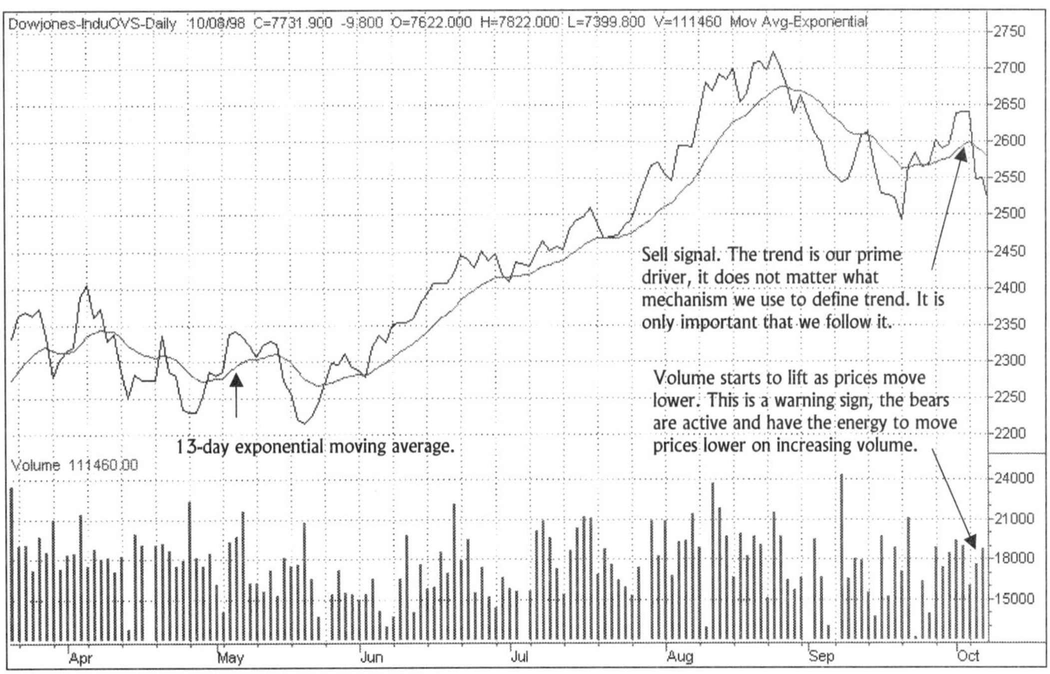

TRADING RULE

The market will tell you which direction to face. You will tell it at your own peril.

> **"If everybody thinks it is going to be a short-lived phenomenon, watch your head."**

Moving forward another few days (Fig. 3.3), we are still short the market. Our primary trend indicator is still pointing south and volume in the market is still rising on downside moves. It is at this stage that we need to consider the prevailing psychology of the market at the time. It was conventional wisdom that the market would not crash until 1988 (how the figure of 1988 was arrived at escapes me). It was thought any slippage from the high was merely a transient development. Notice the similarity with the market of 1998: it was thought that rising stock prices would go on forever. Remember our rule about the herd being wrong. If everybody thinks it is going to be a short-lived phenomenon, watch your head.

FIG. 3.3 – DOW JONES INDEX WITH 13-DAY MOVING AVERAGE

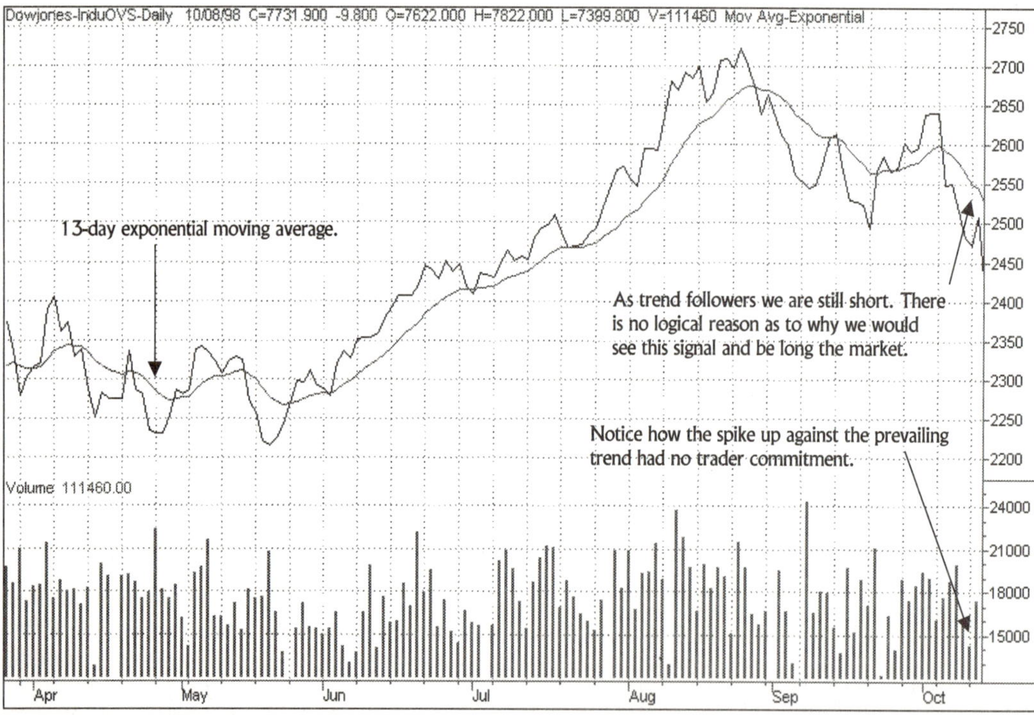

Simple trend and volume analysis has confirmed our decision to be short the market. Our trend indicator has pointed us in the right direction and our review of volume has shown that the bulls lack sufficient force to move prices against the prevailing trend. We are not crash-hunting, we are simply trackers who are astute enough to read the signs. There are no surprises.

FIG. 3.4 – DOW JONES INDEX: DAY BEFORE CRASH

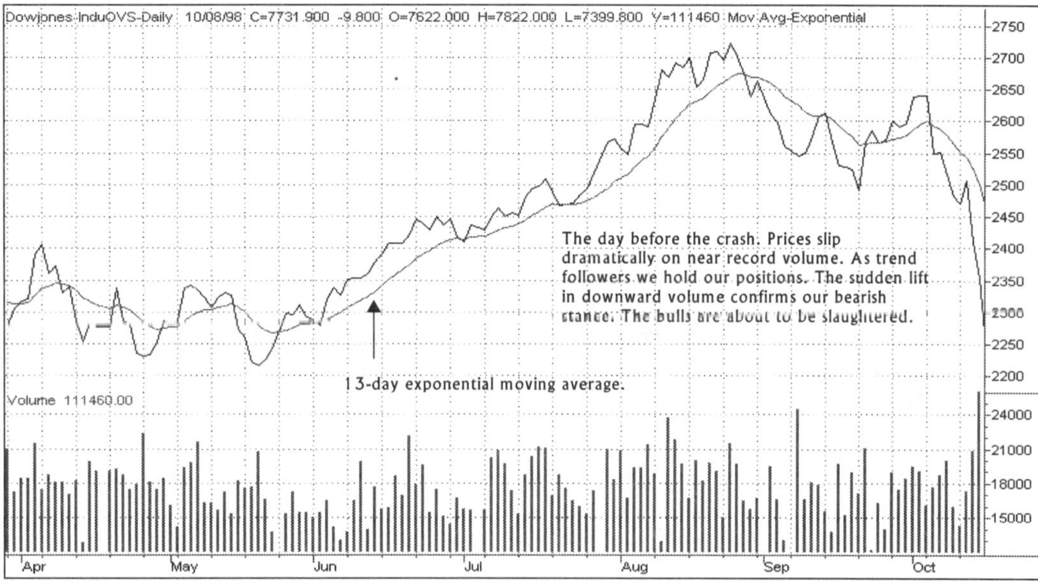

It is the day before the crash (Fig. 3.4). Prices slip dramatically, yet most commentators are still calling it a technical correction and a wonderful buying opportunity. The music is about to stop, and the majority of market participants, despite the warning signs, will be unable to find a chair.

FIG. 3.5 – DOW JONES INDEX: DAY OF CRASH

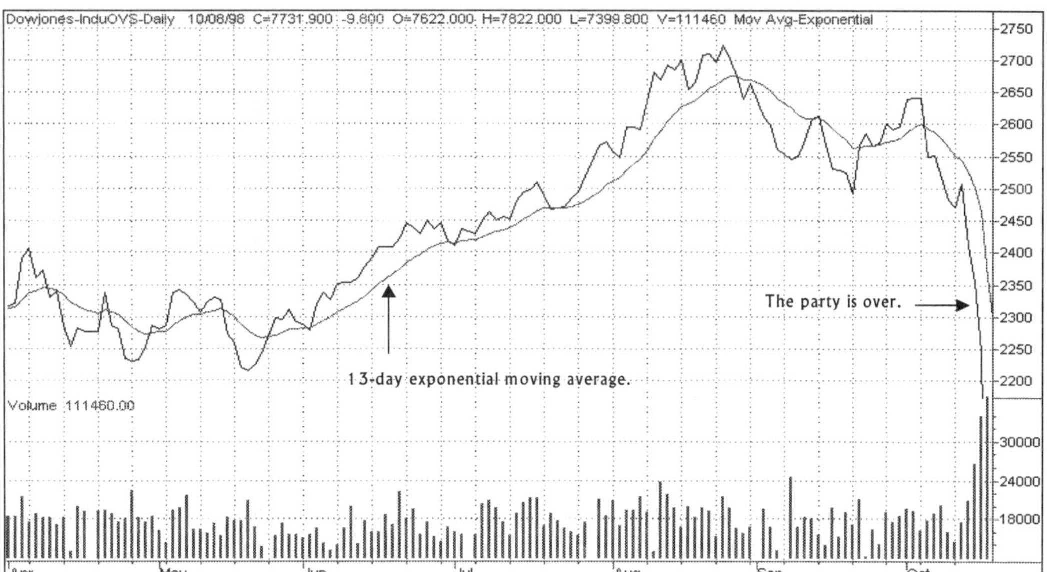

Our decision to be on the short side of the market is confirmed in spectacular fashion as the market literally falls out of bed (Fig. 3.5). The bull run of the 1980s is over.

Reality Check

Anyone who was short the actual crash got lucky, not in their decision to be short the market but rather in terms of the magnitude of the fall. Many indicators pointed to the market being intrinsically unstable and unable to sustain itself for much longer, but, as we said before, these indicators are imprecise and need to be backed up by more delicate forms of analysis. The decision to be short the market was correct based upon the simple methodology we have reviewed. A similar picture arises when we view the local market in the week leading up to the crash.

Closer to Home

In reviewing the local market, I want to look at the sell signals we would receive in such a volatile market. This chart (Fig. 3.6) shows the All Ordinaries Index at the end of September 1987. We can see a clear sell signal on 23 September. The oscillator histogram has generated a bearish divergence. Price has moved to a new all-time high but the oscillator has failed to move beyond its previous record high (refer to Chapter 5 for an explanation of the oscillator histogram).

FIG. 3.6 – ALL ORDINARIES INDEX

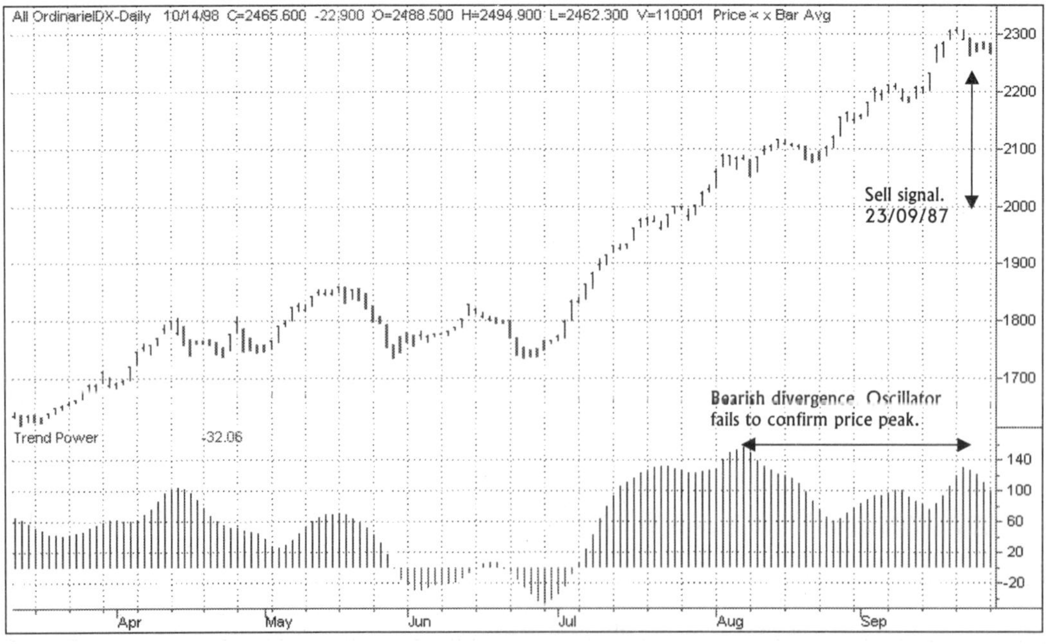

FIG. 3.7 – ALL ORDINARIES WITH SRSI

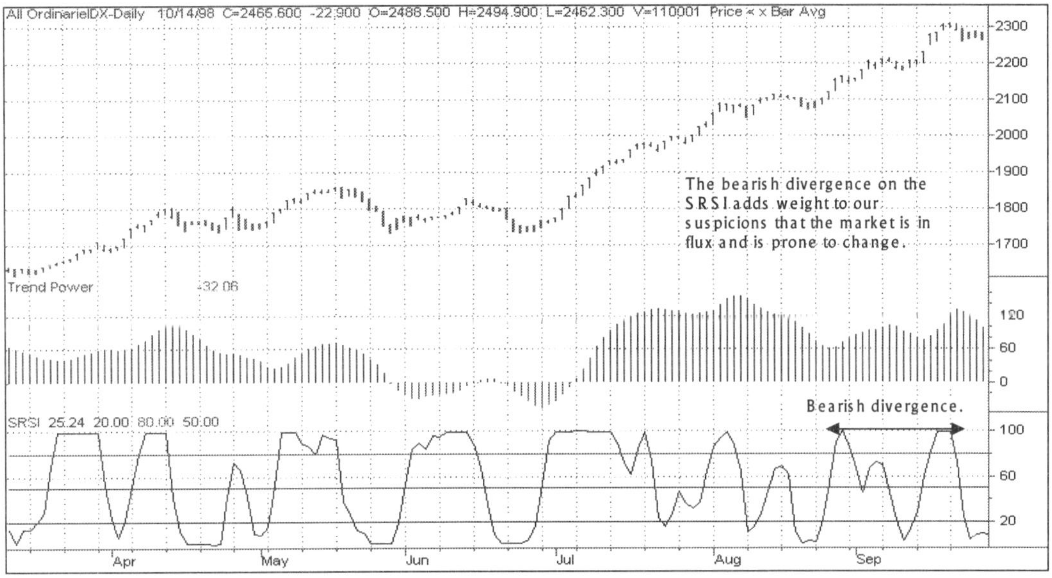

The market is now flashing an amber light, warning us the psychology of traders is unstable. This perception of instability is heightened by a secondary divergence that is generated when we apply the SRSI (Stochastic Relative Strength Indicator) (Fig. 3.7). The application of the RSI (Relative Strength Indicator) also generates a bearish divergence (Fig. 3.8). The evidence that we should be short the market is compelling (refer to Chapter 5 for an explanation of these indicators).

FIG. 3.8 – ALL ORDINARIES WITH RSI

If we move forward to the day preceding the crash, we can see that our sell signal has persisted (Fig. 3.9). As was the case with our analysis of the Dow, the market has told us what direction to face. There is no conceivable reason for us to be long the market. Such a decision would simply be nonsensical and would fly in the face of the evidence we have seen.

I have included the chart below on the All Ordinaries for instructive purposes. It shows the value of listening to the market. We did not predict the crash, but in this situation we would have been facing the right direction.

FIG. 3.9 – ALL ORDINARIES: DAY BEFORE CRASH

As further evidence that all we need to do is listen to the markets, I have included charts of BHP (Fig. 3.10) and NCP (Fig. 3.11). In both charts I have highlighted when the sell signals were given (downtick bars and accelerating downtrend – see Chapter 5). BHP gave a sell signal on 23 September 1987, the same day as the All Ordinaries, while NCP produced a sell signal on 7 October 1987. A review of the top stocks of this period gives similar signals. It is difficult to find a stock that was giving a buy signal going into the crash. This leads us to a very important point: crashes do not occur like bolts from the blue. You will never encounter a situation where you go to bed with the market hitting a new record high only to have it halve the next day. Markets have a tendency to unwind from their highs and then accelerate into a decline. Consequently, indicators will foreshadow a fall. The only people who do not expect a shake-out in the market are those who do not listen to it, which is why as a serious trader you need to develop a means of interpreting price action against the broad backdrop of macro indicators. The point you should take from this section is to always obey your system.

FIG. 3.10 – BHP (1987)

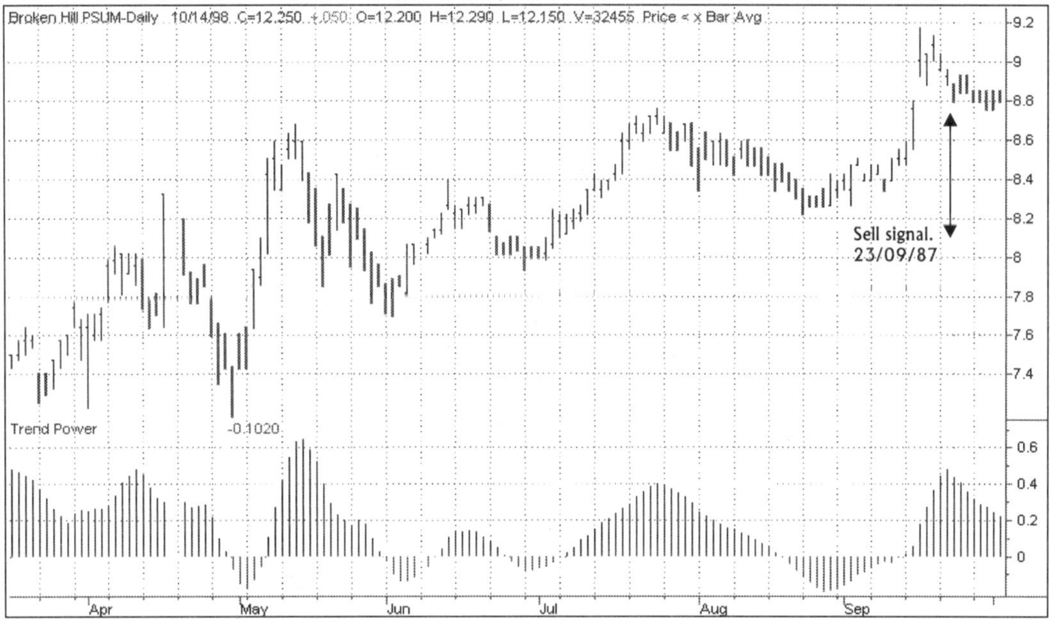

FIG. 3.11 – NCP (1987)

HINDSIGHT AS AN INVESTMENT TOOL

Looking backwards can be a useful guide, but it will not tell us what is going to happen – it will only tell us what is *likely* to happen. To help us define periods during which the market may become unstable and likely to reverse, we need to develop a checklist that builds a picture of the market.

Macro Features Of The Market

- *What are the broad fundamentals of the market?* Are average P/E ratios and dividend yields at levels that are historically unsustainable. (For an example of this, the next chapter contains charts of average market P/E ratios and dividend yield.)
- *Are you hearing a lot of people talk about the stock market?* As J.P. Morgan is once reputed to have said, when the local shoe-shine boys begin to talk about their share portfolios it is time to sell. This is a broad indicator for the level of public involvement in the market. Markets with a very high degree of public involvement are very unstable: for example, the October 1987 crash and the recent crashes in Asia. The general public approaches the stock market as if it were an elevator that only went one way. Due to their naiveté and the misinformation they receive they are willing to take a much higher degree of risk than would normally be prudent. Paradoxically, the general public have the least tolerance for risk, so while they are willing to push prices higher they will also take flight at the first hint of trouble.

  This can be seen if we review the role of volume in the phases of the market. During phase three – the consolidation phase after an uptrend – there were often volume spikes. These spikes are the last of the bulls and, by and large, they are members of the general public (and fund managers) who are unwilling to accept that prices are not on an ever-upwardly spiralling circuit. This attitude results in climax buying, which is the large volume spikes seen before prices decline.

  The tendency of the general public to panic after the event can also be seen in the high volumes that occur at the bottom of downward moves. This climax selling is literally the reverse of the buying seen in terminal consolidation phases. The general public traditionally do their buying at the top and selling at the bottom.

  My own experience of this comes from a purchase of a set of tyres for my car. The young man selling me the tyres was elucidating on his decision to enter the market, and all the reasons why he thought the market was going up. In addition to this, the suburb where I live in Melbourne receives a free glossy magazine, pompously titled *Inside Melbourne*. This magazine concerns itself with what hairdresser has moved from one end of Toorak Road to the other, or how best to prepare aubergines for your next cocktail party. Yet in April 1998, its lead story was about the sharemarket and all the reasons you did not want to miss out. While these points may seem trivial, they illustrate that the last phase of a bull market is controlled by an overwhelming involvement of the general public. The general public have both the least tolerance of risk and the greatest level of misunderstanding of the market.

- *Are there a large number of floats on offer, each one of lower quality than the last?* Is the market flooded with new schemes for high technology, biotechnology and plain-silly ideas like ostrich farming? When these types of companies start to use the stock market as their prime source of venture capital, you can be assured the market has reached a stage of mania that is the terminal phase of every market. It is also worth noting that when you hear the expression "venture capital" bandied about it is time to be concerned.
- *Do you see a large number of advertisements for systems for trading the stock market, each of which promises astronomical returns for very little effort?* These promoters come out of the woodwork during bull markets, and disappear just as quickly when the market falters.
- *Is the current mantra among the investing community: "this time it's different"?* This has been the long-held dogma of everyone who earns a buck by selling second-hand goods, which is what your stockbroker does. If you think that booms are a new thing then you should learn a little about history – familiarise yourself with the South Sea Bubble, the Dutch tulip boom and the financial crisis that gripped the Holy Roman Empire from 1618 to 1623. For an excellent run-down of the mechanics of booms and busts, you must read *Manias, Panics and Crashes* by Charles P. Kindleberger.

"Is the current mantra among the investing community: *'this time it's different'*?"

- *Is the market not responding to positive news as it once did?* Is the market prone to move down on bad or indifferent news, whereas in the past it would have remained unchanged?
- *Is the crowd saying a crash is imminent?* If the ill-informed are making a concrete prediction, then they are more often than not wrong. If there is a correction it will be a two-day wonder: for example, the October 1997 crash. If you don't believe that the herd does not know what it is talking about, consider the simple statistic that more than 80% of people who trade derivatives lose money consistently.

TREND AND SENTIMENT ANALYSIS

Examining the broad features of the market gives us an imprecise indication of the state of the market. In no way does it give us adequate information upon which to make a decision regarding trading. Merely looking at macro features is the equivalent of looking out the window and seeing that the sun is shining, and from this fact trying to deduce what the temperature is. If you were enduring an Alaskan winter, it is quite possible that it is bright and sunny yet freezing outside. If you were in the Northern Territory, however, the opposite may apply – it could be hot enough to melt bitumen. In either instance, merely looking out the window does not provide enough information to make an informed judgement. For this reason, we need to develop a checklist that examines the actual dynamics of price-action and, from there, develop an idea of the actual trend of the market.

Trends

➡ *What is the trend of the prices?* We never, irrespective of what our broad indicators say, attempt to trade in the opposite direction to the prevailing trend. The trend is what is actually happening with price – it is the reality of a particular moment. Our macro indicators merely act as a backdrop to this.

Trends can easily be defined by the use of a moving average. Since we are interested in mid-term swings in market sentiment, we should use a 13-day moving average. Such a time span filters out some of the whipsaw effect that is common with shorter-term moving averages.

Many traders, when trying to detect a change in trend, try to use a moving average that is too short. It is difficult to trade substantial moves in a trend with anything less than a 13-day moving average. Some traders I have encountered attempt to trade with time periods as low as five days. Such a time scale is impossible to use for the purposes of trying to determine major shifts in sentiment. We are not interested in whether today's closing price is lower than yesterday's. We want to know if this week's close is lower than last week's. Portfolio traders may wish to look at weekly data to time their entries.

Sentiment

➡ *What is the sentiment of the market?* Are your oscillators highlighting a divergence between price and sentiment? If so, then you are getting an amber light as to the potential for change.

- *Has volatility increased rapidly?* This signifies that a change in trend is imminent. It gives us no idea of the possible duration of this change, but it is an early warning signal.
- *What is the SRSI telling you about who is in charge?* Are bears able to close prices at the lower edge of each trading range, or are bulls merely fatigued and prices are drifting back?
- *What is happening with the RSI?* Is it confirming moves in the market, or is there a divergence between price and sentiment building? Divergences between price and sentiment lead to brittle markets that can decline very quickly.
- *Is there selling volume in the market?* On days when the market closes down, is the volume higher than on days when the market closes up? This was a key indicator in the days leading up to the 1987 crash – down-moves were severe and accompanied by a lift in volume, whereas up-moves had very little trader involvement.

PART II

BEAR TAMING

"Stocks are now at what looks like a permanently high plateau."

ECONOMIST IRVING FISHER, THE WEEK BEFORE THE 1929 CRASH

4: THE BIG PICTURE

THE TASK FOR a bear is to anticipate the formation of a bear market. More importantly, it is to anticipate the sudden breakdown and sentiment reversals that accompany the end of bull markets. The reasons for this are obvious: it enables you to exit your bullish positions before the market reverses, and it allows you to take advantage of the sudden down-swings in the market.

Markets never change, because the people who make up markets are incapable of change. History repeats itself in a never-ending cycle (for those of you who doubt this, go to *Memoirs of Extraordinary Popular Delusions and the Madness of Crowds* by Charles Mackay and read the summarised version of various crashes throughout history). Simply stating this, however, is of no value to us unless we have some form of analysis to guide us. As traders, our analysis should start with an examination of history in order to pinpoint any levels at which markets may become unstable. Such an analysis acts as an early warning system, alerting us to possible changes in the mood of the herd that makes up each market.

In Australia, all analysis of equity markets starts with an analysis of US markets. As the old adage says: if Wall Street sneezes, we catch a cold. Any analysis must focus on the trend of the two major US indices: the S&P500 and the Dow Jones Index. (The Dow Jones Index is used to monitor the performance of the American stock market. The Dow is a very narrow measure, consisting of only the top 30 stocks. The S&P500 is a broader index than the Dow. While both are used to gauge the performance of the American stock market, the S&P500 includes the top 500 stocks, so it is more representative of the market as a whole.)

However, our analysis of the markets is not simply a matter of putting up a chart and saying what part of the cycle the market is in and acting accordingly. We need to build up a picture of the market, which will act as a backdrop to the analytical techniques that will be investigated later.

MARKET CYCLES IN THE UNITED STATES

In trading, all the information we are exposed to is historical. When we look at a chart, we are looking at the past to make judgements about the future. The paradox of this is that the decisions we are making are never reflected on either a chart or a simple print-out of price data. We operate in the present, yet all our data by definition can only represent the past. This does not, however, diminish the value of historical data in providing evidence of possible changes in markets or potential insights into how long these changes may last.

As we have seen, market cycles can be fairly chaotic. There appears to be no fixed cycle to market activity on a broad scale. However, we can examine our history of markets to gain an insight into how long within a given range each of our cycles may last. If we consider the table opposite (Table 4.1) – which is an historical analysis of the bull and bear market cycles in the US from 1796 to 1990 – we can get an idea as to the average intensity of each decline. Whilst we are not attempting to use this data to predict either a starting or finishing date for a bear market, it does allow us to make reasoned judgements as to the possible length of each cycle.

"Once again it becomes apparent that bull and bear markets differ not only in intensity but in duration."

A single point is immediately apparent from this information. Bull markets are of much greater intensity in terms of the percentage change in the index. On average, bull markets result in a 105% increase in the underlying index, whereas bear markets yield on average a 36% decrease in the index. We can make a reasoned judgement as to when an index – in this example the S&P500 – may become overheated and due for slippage. This also allows us to make decisions about bear markets and their average intensity. This does not mean we can predict the exit percentage move down of a market, nor does it allow us to make the statement that the market has declined 35% therefore the bear market is over and we can go long. What it does tell us is the intensity of markets when they do move, and it gives us very broad parameters for understanding the markets we are in. These are not timing tools, so as such they will not allow us to make trading decisions, but this information will add to our understanding of markets. Such a model ties in well with our portfolio trading model that we will examine later.

If we examine Table 4.2 (on page 44) we get an idea of the relationship between each cycle. Once again it becomes apparent that bull and bear markets differ not only in intensity but in duration. From the period 1942 to 1994, bull markets lasted an average of 3.11 years, whereas bear markets lasted on average only 0.89 years, a significant difference.

TABLE 4.1 – MARKET CYCLES 1796-1990

MARKET TOP	MARKET BOTTOM	INDEX HIGH	INDEX LOW	% INCREASE	% DECLINE
July 1990	October 1990	369.78	294.51	67.14	20.36
August 1987	December 1987	337.89	221.24	233.09	34.52
November 1980	August 1982	140.52	101.44	61.70	27.81
December 1976	March 1978	107.48	86.90	72.58	19.15
January 1973	October 1974	119.87	62.28	73.00	48.04
November 1968	May 1970	108.37	69.29	40.05	36.06
February 1966	October 1966	94.06	73.20	79.78	22.18
December 1961	June 1962	72.64	52.32	86.35	27.97
August 1956	October 1957	49.74	38.98	267.08	21.63
May 1946	June 1949	19.25	13.55	157.70	29.61
November 1938	April 1942	13.79	7.47	62.24	45.83
March 1937	March 1938	18.68	8.50	131.76	54.50
July 1933	March 1935	12.20	8.06	120.61	33.93
September 1932	February 1933	9.06	5.53	105.91	38.96
September 1929	June 1932	31.86	4.40	393.95	86.19
July 1919	August 1921	9.51	6.45	39.85	32.18
November 1916	December 1917	10.21	6.80	38.91	33.40
December 1909	December 1914	10.30	7.35	64.80	28.64
September 1906	November 1907	10.03	6.25	60.22	37.69
June 1901	October 1903	8.05	6.26	111.29	22.24
January 1893	August 1896	5.61	3.81	21.96	32.09
May 1887	December 1890	5.90	4.60	39.15	22.03
June 1881	January 1885	6.58	4.24	140.15	35.56
May 1872	June 1877	5.19	2.74	61.68	47.21
April 1864	April 1865	4.38	3.21	271.19	26.71
December 1852	October 1857	3.33	1.18	46.70	64.56
August 1847	November 1848	2.94	2.27	87.26	22.79
May 1835	January 1843	3.61	1.57	64.09	56.51
December 1802	August 1829	3.20	2.20	51.66	31.25
February 1796	September 1798	3.02	2.11	N/A	30.13

Original data for Table 4.1 supplied by Global Financial Data, 500 North Atlantic, Suite 208, Alhambra, CA 91801

TABLE 4.2 – MARKET CYCLES 1942-1994

DATE	S&P500 VALUE	WHERE IN CYCLE	BULL MARKET CHANGE (%)	YEARS IN BULL MARKET	BEAR MARKET CHANGE (%)	YEARS IN BEAR MARKET	CYCLE CHANGE (%)	YEARS IN CYCLE
28/04/42	7.47	Low						
29/05/46	19.25	High	157.70	4.08				
09/10/46	14.12	Low			-26.65	0.36	89.02	4.45
15/06/48	17.06	High	20.82	1.68				
13/06/49	13.55	Low			-20.57	0.99	-4.04	2.68
05/01/53	26.66	High	96.75	3.56				
14/09/53	22.71	Low			-14.82	0.69	67.60	4.25
02/08/56	49.74	High	119.02	2.88				
22/10/57	38.98	Low			-21.63	1.22	71.64	4.10
12/12/61	72.64	High	86.35	4.14				
26/06/62	52.32	Low			-27.97	0.54	34.22	4.68
09/02/66	94.06	High	79.78	3.62				
07/10/66	73.20	Low			-22.18	0.66	39.91	4.28
29/11/68	108.37	High	48.05	2.15				
26/05/70	69.29	Low			-36.06	1.49	-5.34	3.63
11/01/73	120.24	High	73.53	2.63				
03/10/74	62.28	Low			-48.20	1.72	-10.12	4.36
21/09/76	107.83	High	73.14	1.97				
06/03/78	86.90	Low			-19.41	1.45	39.53	3.42
28/11/80	140.52	High	61.70	2.73				
12/08/82	102.42	Low			-27.11	1.70	17.86	4.44
25/08/87	336.77	High	228.81	5.03				
04/12/87	223.92	Low			-33.51	0.28	118.63	5.31
16/07/90	368.95	High	64.77	2.61				
11/10/90	295.46	Low			-19.92	0.24	31.95	2.85
02/02/94	482.00	High	63.14	3.31				
04/04/94	438.92	Low			-8.94	0.17	48.55	3.48

Original data for Table 4.2 supplied by Harry Rood, HR Consultants, http://cpcug.org:80/user/invest/cycledat.html

Remember, this is not a timing tool, it is merely part of our package of background knowledge that enables us to understand how markets function. However, I need to make a point about definitions. In both of these examples, a bear market was considered to be an average decline of 15% or more in the S&P500.

The charts below highlight the 1929-33 bear market (Fig. 4.1) and the 1973-75 bear market (Fig. 4.2). Both of these periods are considered to be representative of bear markets this century, and they adequately demonstrate the ferocity of a bear market. The question passive investors would need to ask is how would they cope with such a markct. What tools would they have in their arsenal to deliver them a positive return during this period? The answer to this question is simple – the passive investor has no methodology for dealing with such a downturn.

FIG. 4.1 – DOW MONTHLY

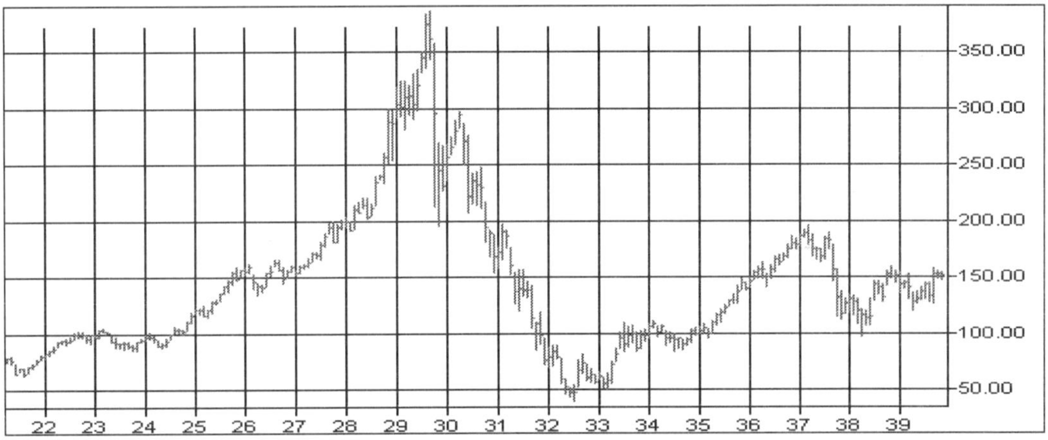

FIG. 4.2 – S&P500 WEEKLY

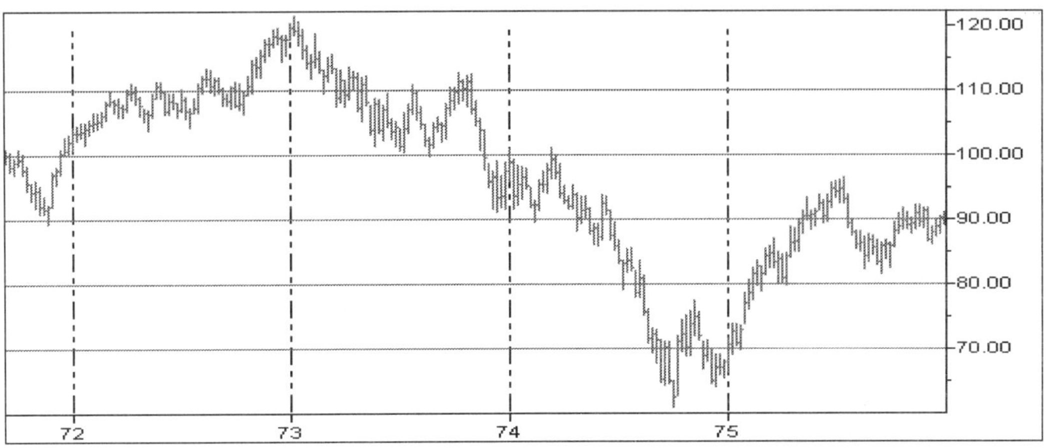

Market Drift

The definition of a bear market used in the previous tables is much stricter than my definition, and it does not take into consideration periods of extensive drift. To reinforce this drift, consider the following chart of the S&P500.

FIG. 4.3 – S&P500 RETURN

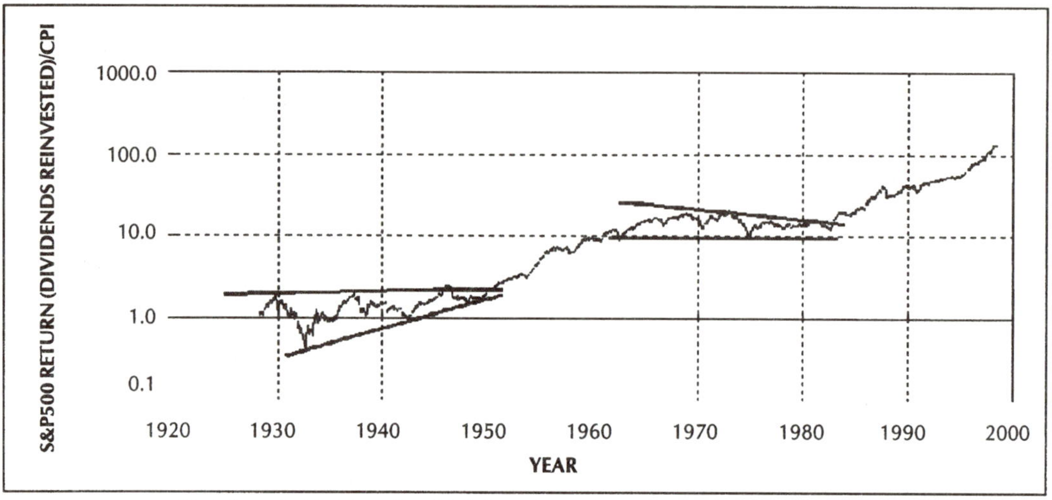

Fig. 4.3 supplied by Harry Rood, HR Consultants, http://cpcug.org:80/user/invest/

This chart has been corrected for inflation. In essence, it measures the index in constant dollar terms. As can be seen, there are extensive periods where the index offers no real return to long-term passive investors. This chart highlights my reasoning as to why a bear market is defined as any period where the market is not advancing. If the market is not advancing and you are a passive investor, then your are – by my definition – caught in a bear market.

If you are strictly a passive investor who has taken on board the myth that the market always goes up, when you encounter these prolonged periods of drift you will see a serious erosion in the real spending power of your money. A market that drifts for 10 to 15 years may not seem to present much of a problem, but consider that most people's long-term investment horizon is 10 to 15 years. This point takes on even more relevance when you consider the current push to self-funding for retirees. How will your superannuation nest-egg look if you get no growth from your portfolio for ten years? Passive investing offers you no methodology for coping with such markets, and it should be avoided at all costs. All investing is trading, and as such it requires an active approach to the market. Grasping for your talisman will not help you make money in tough times.

> **"October is one of the perculiarly dangerous months to speculate in stocks. The others are January, July, September, April, November, May, March, June, December, August and February."**
>
> *MARK TWAIN, 1894*

THE MYTH OF OCTOBER

One would think that financial markets are the bastion of rational thought, that only ideas and concepts that have any basis in fact would be absorbed into the culture of trading. Unfortunately this isn't the case. There are as many superstitions in trading as there are in horse racing or the picking of lottery numbers. One of the most prevalent myths is that the month of October holds some special importance to traders. The belief is that by some strange conjunction of the planets or a clustering of full moons the market will turn around and head south every October, as if it were some sort of confused duck. Fortunately such a hypothesis is easily tested, and to do this we should look at the global index generated by Global Financial Data (Table 4.3). We will then turn our attention to the domestic market (Table 4.4).

The following table tracks the worst percentage declines on record for the global index.

The instant response of people upon viewing this data is to say that October features three times in Table 4.3 – surely this is significant. The simple answer to this is no, it isn't. Such an interpretation of the data is simplistic and lacks any understanding of statistical information. Consider the number of times October has not figured in downturns in the market. Since organised stock markets have been trading there are literally hundreds of Octobers where the market has done nothing special at all. The market doing something special in October on three of those occasions out of literally hundreds ranks merely as an interesting curiosity. It is, however, nothing more than coincidence. (As an aside, traders must understand the power of coincidence to upset rational thinking. Consider the myth that the phone rings more often when you are in the shower. Because having to get out of the shower to answer the phone ranks as a memorable or unusual event, this event assumes unnatural importance. But think of the thousands of times you have been in the shower and the phone has not rung. Coincidence is not correlation, and certainly should not be a basis for trading decisions.)

TABLE 4.3 – GLOBAL INDEX WORST DECLINES

WORST MONTH	PERCENTAGE RETURN
September 1931	-18.16%
October 1987	-17.12%
January 1946	-16.51%
November 1973	-13.15%
December 1931	-11.65%
March 1980	-11.06%
May 1940	-10.82%
September 1990	-10.75%
October 1990	-10.61%
August 1974	-10.21%
October 1929	-10.00%

Original data for Tables 4.3 and 4.4 supplied by Global Financial Data, 500 North Atlantic, Suite 208, Alhambra, CA 91801

If we look at Table 4.4, once again we see that October has no special place in the calendar of traders when it is considered in the overall scheme of things. It is interesting to note that October has only assumed a special importance since 1987. It is interesting to speculate on the role of information – or misinformation – and its ability to permeate the minds of traders. Crowds are homogenous, and will take on whatever the prevailing belief system is if it is presented forcefully enough, or if there is no critical judgement made about the veracity of the information being presented. If you doubt the power of popular myths, consider the fact that many Americans believe they have been the victim of alien abduction, or the power astrology has over some people despite being totally discredited.

TABLE 4.4 – ALL ORDINARIES WORST DECLINES

WORST MONTH	PERCENTAGE RETURN
October 1987	-42.51%
October 1875	-19.16%
July 1974	-14.86%
May 1974	-14.44%
March 1980	-14.19%
May 1984	-13.39%
September 1968	-13.31%
January 1876	-12.28%
November 1930	-12.08%
December 1896	-10.96%

P/E Ratios

FIG. 4.4 – S&P500 P/E RATIO

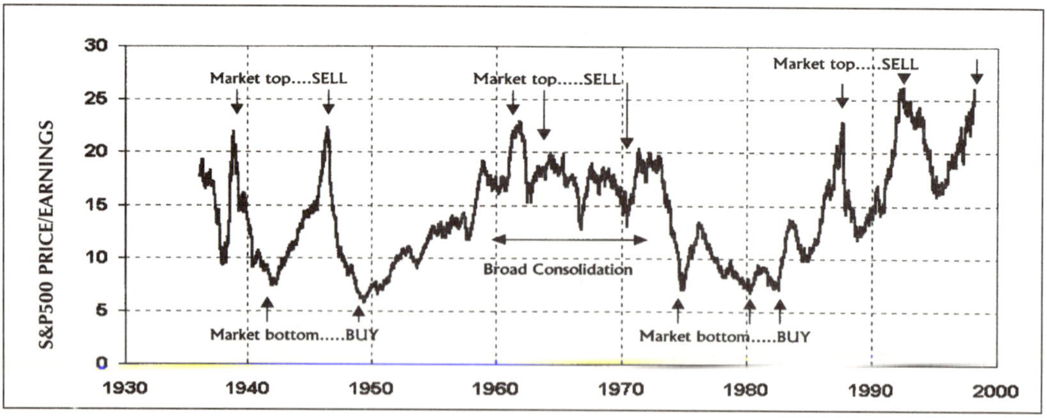

This chart (Fig. 4.4) is of the S&P500 Price-to-Earnings (P/E) ratio. P/E ratios are an indicator of the health of the market – they are much like a barometer. They are calculated by dividing the current market price by earnings. The interpretation of this chart is relatively simple. Periods of high P/Es indicate that market participants are chasing up the value of stocks, and this lift in price is not being met by a commensurate lift in earnings. Under a traditional interpretation, when the market has a high P/E ratio it is said to be expensive or overvalued. We have to be very careful, however, about using emotive terms such as expensive or overvalued. They are value judgements, and we are only interested in facts. A more accurate interpretation is to say that markets *always* reverse from extreme P/E ratios.

This tool is a good psychological barometer. In times of low P/Es, stocks are friendless and are ignored by the herd. This represents an excellent buying opportunity for the portfolio trader. Conversely, during periods of high P/Es stocks are chased by everybody, and there is widespread public involvement in the stock market. Remember, though: the herd is always wrong.

TRADING RULE

If the herd thinks something is a good long-term proposition, then it is probably, at best, a reasonable short-term proposition.

The traditional interpretation of this P/E chart, particularly during sustained bull runs, is that it is an indication that the market is about to suddenly reverse and drop like a stone. Such an interpretation is somewhat simplistic: a more appropriate interpretation is to say that, on the balance of probabilities, the market has entered a phase where, historically, it is unstable, and that prices are unsustainable at current levels. You will note from this chart that prices can maintain relatively high levels for some time before the market eventually reverses, hence, as an indicator, this is somewhat imprecise in its timing. Markets always reverse from their highs: high P/Es are unsustainable.

The table below shows how P/E ratios affect the performance of stocks.

TABLE 4.5 – PERFORMANCE OF STOCKS ACCORDING TO P/E RANKING (APRIL 1957-MARCH 1971)

P/E QUINTILE	AVERAGE % PRICE INCREASES PER YEAR	BETA (SYSTEMATIC RISK)
A (Highest)	9.3	1.1121
B	9.3	1.0387
C	11.7	0.9678
D	13.6	0.9401
E (Lowest)	16.3	0.9866

Dividend Yield

Table 4.6 illustrates the role that dividend yield plays in the psychological health of the market. As can be seen, there is a fairly simple relationship between dividend levels and the probability of a rise in prices. This relationship can be stated as: a decrease in dividends leads to a decrease in the probability of prices rising in the following year. At the time of writing, the dividend yield on the S&P500 was at an historically low 2%. Again, this does not automatically indicate that a correction in the bull market is imminent, and that we are about to enter a new dark age merely because certain indices have reached historic reversal points. Remember, markets can hold extreme values for some time before reversing, but they always reverse.

TABLE 4.6 – DIVIDEND YIELDS AND STOCK PRICES (1941-75)

DOW JONES DIVIDEND YIELD	S&P500 INDEX ONE YEAR LATER	PROBABILITY OF RISING PRICES
Under 3%	−10.1%	0%
3.0% – 4.0%	+2.0%	59%
4.0% – 6.0%	+11.4%	72%
6.0% – 7.0%	+15.0%	87%
Over 7.0%	+37.8%	100%
35-Year Average	+7.7%	68%

Closer to Home

The use of such tools gives us a general picture of the health of a market. While there is a correlation between the US markets and our own domestic market, we need to start to narrow our focus to see if the local market has been following the same course.

As can be seen from the chart of the average P/E ratio for the All Ordinaries Index (Fig. 4.5), a similar pattern emerges to that of the US markets we have examined. There are historical levels at which the market becomes unstable and the probability of a reversal increases – a reversal is probable, but not imminent. Our interpretation of this chart, if we were worried about the slowing of a bull market, would be that, on an historical basis, the market is fragile. Investors have lifted prices to a point at which they are traditionally unsustainable. Such an interpretation would be reason for portfolio investors to lighten their market weighting substantially. However, such a chart is not a signal to go short the market and adopt an aggressive bearish stance without some further analysis.

FIG. 4.5 – AVERAGE P/E RATIO FOR ALL ORDINARIES

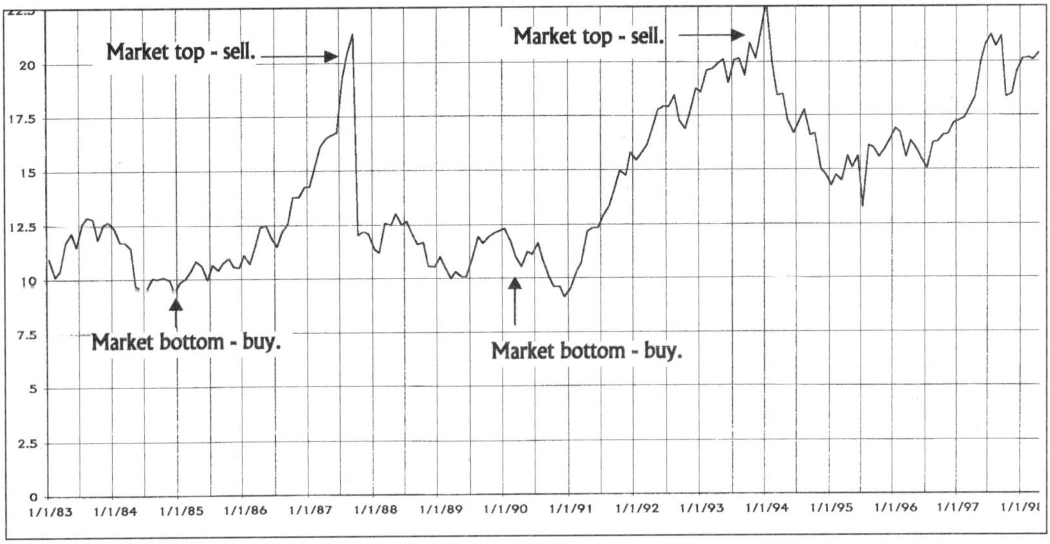

This chart (Fig. 4.6) is of the average dividend yield on the All Ordinaries Index. A similar pattern emerges. There are historical levels at which the market becomes unstable and reversals are likely in the future. However, as we saw before, estimating the timing of these reversals based upon these very broad indicators is imprecise, and needs to be supplemented by additional information in the form of trend analysis. In this next section, it will help if you are familiar with technical analysis, or charting as it is more often referred to. (For more information on charting, see my book, *The Art of Trading*, published by Wrightbooks.)

FIG. 4.6 – AVERAGE DIVIDEND YIELD FOR ALL ORDINARIES

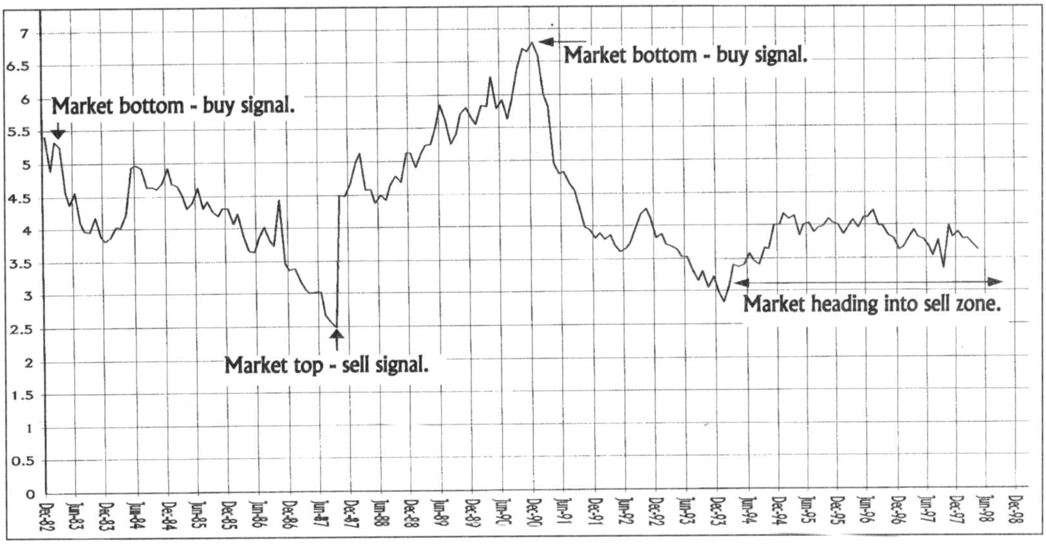

5: DESIGNING A BEAR MARKET TRADING SYSTEM

SO FAR WE have only made broad assumptions about the health of the market. Whilst macro indicators such as overall market P/E and dividend yield are useful signposts, they do not provide sufficient discrimination to allow us to time our entry into and exit from the market. The trading techniques that are explored later in this book are reliant upon timing. The aim of this chapter is to help you design a trading system to allow the specific timing of trades. To do this, we are going to go through some basic indicators, beginning with simple trend and volume analysis, followed by an examination of how sentiment and divergences between price and sentiment can give us an early warning signal. Finally we will look at a break-out system.

> **"The great mistake is to anticipate the outcome of an engagement. Let nature take its course and your tools will strike at the right moment."**
>
> *BRUCE LEE*

Most traders, when faced with the prospect of designing a trading system, immediately reach for the most powerful software they can find. There is a prevailing belief among traders that bigger, more complicated and more expensive is better. Unfortunately such belief holds no basis in fact. If it did, all the money would be made by the people with the most expensive software. I havc seen no evidence that paying $5,000 for a piece of software makes you ten times more profitable than someone who paid $500. In fact, my own experience seems to indicate that the opposite is true.

The same situation applies to indicators. Traders, out of habit, reach for what they perceive to be the most powerful analytical tools in their arsenal. In this chapter, we are going to take a slightly different approach.

We are going to look at only five basic tools:

1 Trendlines
2 Moving averages
3 RSI and divergences
4 SRSI and divergences
5 Break-out trading systems.

TRENDLINES

Before beginning our analysis of trendlines, it is necessary to make a few basic points about the way trendlines are applied.

Trendlines are our most basic trading tool. They can be plotted using a linear scale or the more common logarithmic scale (I choose to use a linear scale). They require no expensive software, only the ability to plot prices. They can even be drawn by hand. It is their simplicity that gives them their power, yet once again many traders attempt to complicate matters by either drawing trendlines incorrectly, drawing too many trendlines or concentrating on what trendlines told them in the dim dark past rather than what they can tell them about current price action.

Mistake Number 1: Drawing Trendlines Incorrectly

Many traders panic at the thought of drawing trendlines. They suffer vapour-lock trying to decide what points to connect. In drawing trendlines, our major concern is to highlight pivot shifts in trader psychology. We then want to see whether these shifts are confirmed by accessory moves. In a downtrend, we connect the two major pivots. These may be separated by a few days. It is these pivots that will form the basis for the remainder of the trend. If we refer to the example of ANZ (Fig. 5.1, opposite) we can see that the bulk of the trend was defined by the first two downward moves of the trend. Later moves merely confirmed these two initial moves.

"In drawing trendlines, our major concern is to highlight pivot shifts in trader psychology."

Mistake Number 2: Drawing Too Many Trendlines

Once a trader starts scribbling trendlines all over a chart, it is tempting to keep going. The resultant picture looks something akin to an aerial photograph of the Melbourne tram network, and is by and large completely useless to the trader. Simple is best. If you cannot see what is happening with one or two trendlines, five or ten will not help.

Mistake Number 3: The Lure Of The Left Hand Side

As traders, we are caught in the paradox of having to make decisions about the future based upon information from the past. Many traders try to overcome this difficulty by scribbling all over the left hand side of the chart. This may ease the psychological burden of trading, but it is completely irrelevant. Some trends can carry on for months, and what has happened in the past can influence the future, but we are not trading the left hand side of the chart. To be blunt, we are not even on the chart, since the chart represents history and we are trading the present. It may make traders feel good to go back over the past and scratch their heads wisely when they see connections between past trends, but that does not help them in the here and now.

ANZ Analysis

FIG. 5.1 – ANZ WITH TRENDLINES (1998)

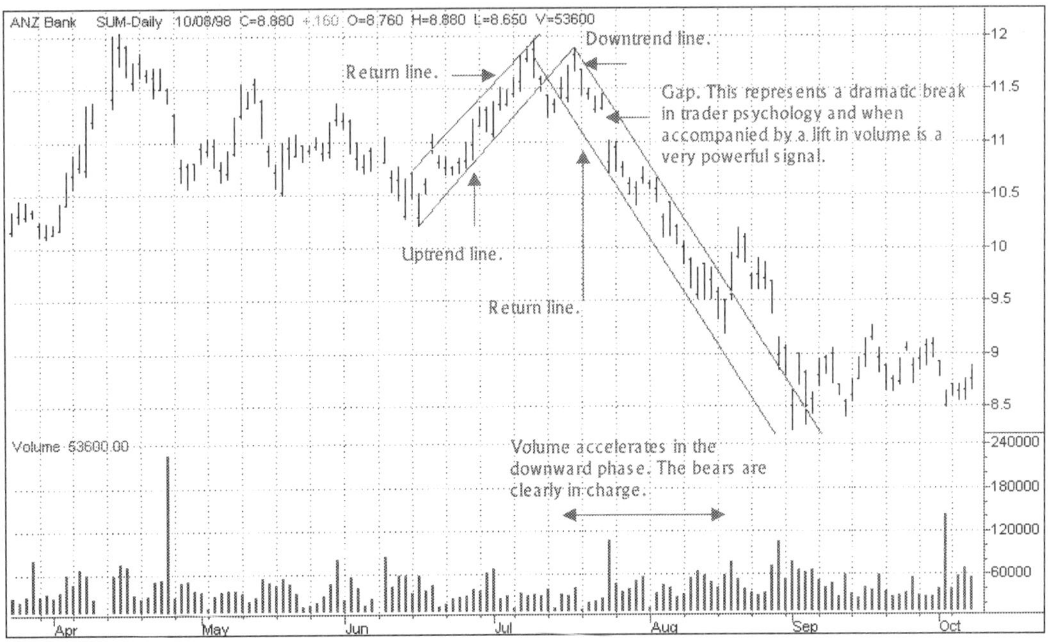

In analysing ANZ, we will set a few ground rules for the interpretation of trendlines:

1 Each trendline must have what is known as a return line. The return line acts as a shadow to the prevailing trend. It is essential to have a return line because it will alert us to breaks in the underlying trend. It will also stop us jumping at shadows because we will be able to gauge the potential dimension of a move away from the

underlying trend. Later in this book we will look at trading congestion zones. It is essential that you get into the habit of plotting return lines. This will add to your chances of survival in congestion areas.

2 Trendlines are of no value unless they are accompanied by a volume indicator. Volume can either confirm or deny a move. Without volume, we will not be able to ascertain the strength of any given move.

In markets that are trending strongly, prices may move from an uptrend to a downtrend without any intervening consolidation. Such swings generally represent powerful changes in market sentiment. This is the situation we see with ANZ: prices move from a four-week uptrend to a sustained downward move. Initially we will concentrate on this transition from uptrend to downtrend – in particular the base of the inverted V formation that signals the oscillation from bull trader opportunity to bear trader opportunity.

It sounds obvious, but it is the termination of the uptrend that determines the initiation of our downtrend. Notice how prices terminate in the uptrend by banging into the return line and then falling. The return line is the point of psychological resistance. It is this point that traders are unwilling to push prices beyond, so we have a clue as to the commitment of traders to the uptrend. A further clue comes from the absence of volume in this terminal phase of the swing. If traders had wanted to push prices beyond the boundaries of the current return line then this would have been accompanied by a surge in volume.

The lift in volume comes as prices fall below the uptrend line. The ascendancy is now moving towards the bears, however the bulls have one last attempt at reasserting their dominance as they push prices to the underside of the uptrend line. This move fails, and prices peak. It is this failure that should alert us to the potential for a downward move. At this stage, if we had any long positions in ANZ we should have closed them out. The market has told us what direction it is heading in. Remember, there are very few surprises in the market. Price and volume will tell us everything we need to know.

The true acceleration of our downtrend begins with the presence of the gap (shown on Fig. 5.1). This is a rapid break in sentiment and, in this instance, it is accompanied by a lift in volume. The trading of gaps is a very efficient tool for bears. The rules are very simple. If the gap is confirmed by a rise in volume then you trade aggressively in the direction of the gap. Gaps are rarely ambiguous in their presentation, and present excellent trading opportunities. In our ANZ example, if we are long at the presentation of the gap then we are facing the wrong direction. The bears are clearly in charge, and the bulls are about to get mauled.

"Gaps are rarely ambiguous in their presentation, and present excellent trading opportunities."

As the initial downtrend terminates, the value of plotting a return line can be seen. Throughout the life of the trend, prices do drift away from the return line, but we have established an upper and lower boundary of price expectation. All trends terminate, and the termination of this downtrend occurs initially in mid-August, as prices break through the downtrend line. This is a clear signal to close out all short positions. Sentiment has turned against the bears. This lift is accompanied by an increase in volume. Once again our volume rules come into play and we need to change our stance away from being bearish. We do not know initially how long this reversal will last, which is why traders should be reactive. The market is again telling us which direction to face – we ignore its instructions at our own peril.

MOVING AVERAGES

Moving averages are by far the most popular tool that traders use. They are, however, quite limited in their usefulness. When traders first encounter moving averages, they believe that they have encountered the Holy Grail. It seems as if all the trader has to do is to buy when the price moves above the moving average and sell when the price moves below the moving average. In essence these are the rules for trading moving averages. However, markets only trend for 20% of their life – the rest of the time they meander in fairly directionless trade. During these periods moving averages are useless.

This brings us to a trading rule for moving averages that the bulk of traders do not understand: if the market is going sideways, using moving averages will cause you to rack up a string of losses. Your Holy Grail in essence becomes a poison chalice. It is essential that you understand this. The only way to adequately deal with directionless markets is to take a step backwards and use trendlines to guide you through the minefield.

If you refer to our ANZ example, you will note that I have converted the chart from a bar chart (Fig. 5.1) to a simple line chart (Fig. 5.2, overleaf). The reason for this is that what happens during the day within the range of a bar chart is essentially meaningless to us when using a moving average. As trend followers, we are only interested in the trend, and the trend is determined by the closing price. Novice traders often believe that there is some sort of special significance to the opening of the market, which is why you often see wild swings in the markets as they open, only to have these perturbations smoothed out during the course of the day. There is an expression in futures trading: *mugs on opening*. The implication is that only amateurs and fools jockey for position during the day. The only thing that really matters is the close, which determines the prevailing trend. The close is ruled by professionals – only amateurs are worried about the opening. The only exception to this is the case of gaps, although gaps are usually only confirmed later in the trading day anyway.

FIG. 5.2 – ANZ WITH MOVING AVERAGE

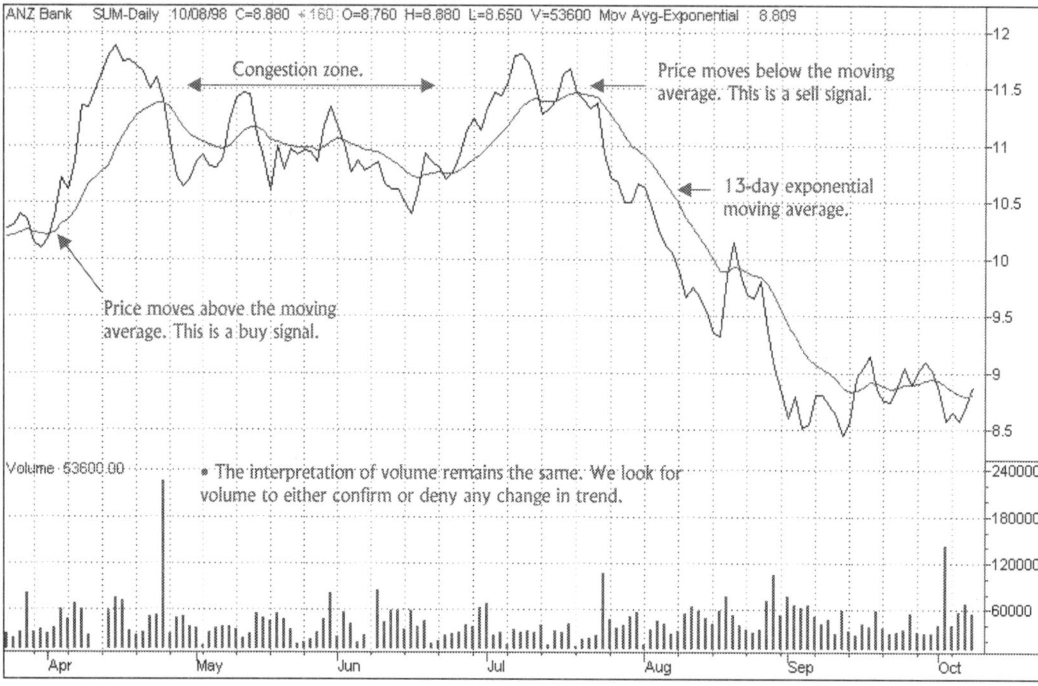

The interpretation of moving averages is very simple, as we have seen, and our ANZ example highlights the conditions for buying and selling. It also highlights the difficulty that moving averages have when the market begins to congest. As a simple rule, if your moving average plateaus, stop using it. The market is going sideways and you are using the wrong tool for the market conditions. It should also be noted that the interpretation of volume remains the same.

RSI DIVERGENCES

The RSI (Relative Strength Index) is an oscillator that measures the strength of an instrument by measuring changes in its closing price. The RSI is a leading indicator, and herein lies its strength. Divergences in price and sentiment as measured by the RSI point to dislocations in the market and trading opportunities.

Most traders use the RSI incorrectly – they use it merely to confirm the direction of the existing trend. If you are using trend-following instruments such as trendlines, moving averages or the MACD histogram then you already know the direction of the trend. You do not need to be told again. The RSI exists to point to possible changes in price dynamics – it warns of impending change.

In the example of the SPI (Fig. 5.3) the RSI is plotted as an overlay of price. Charting programs usually place the oscillator below the chart. This, however, is not always the best way to view the RSI. Plotting it over the chart we are using (see below) enables the easy interpretation of divergences, since a dislocation between price and the RSI is readily apparent. In the example, four divergences have been highlighted – two bearish and two bullish. We are only interested in trading the short side of the market, so we will concentrate on the bearish divergences. Divergences traditionally occur when price and sentiment fail to confirm one another. In our first divergence, price attempts to move beyond its most immediate previous high. The RSI fails to confirm this. From this, we can deduce that prices are in effect weakening and lack the energy to proceed any further in the direction of the prevailing trend. The market confirms this divergence, and the SPI drops approximately 150 points in the next few trading sessions.

FIG. 5.3 – SPI WITH RSI

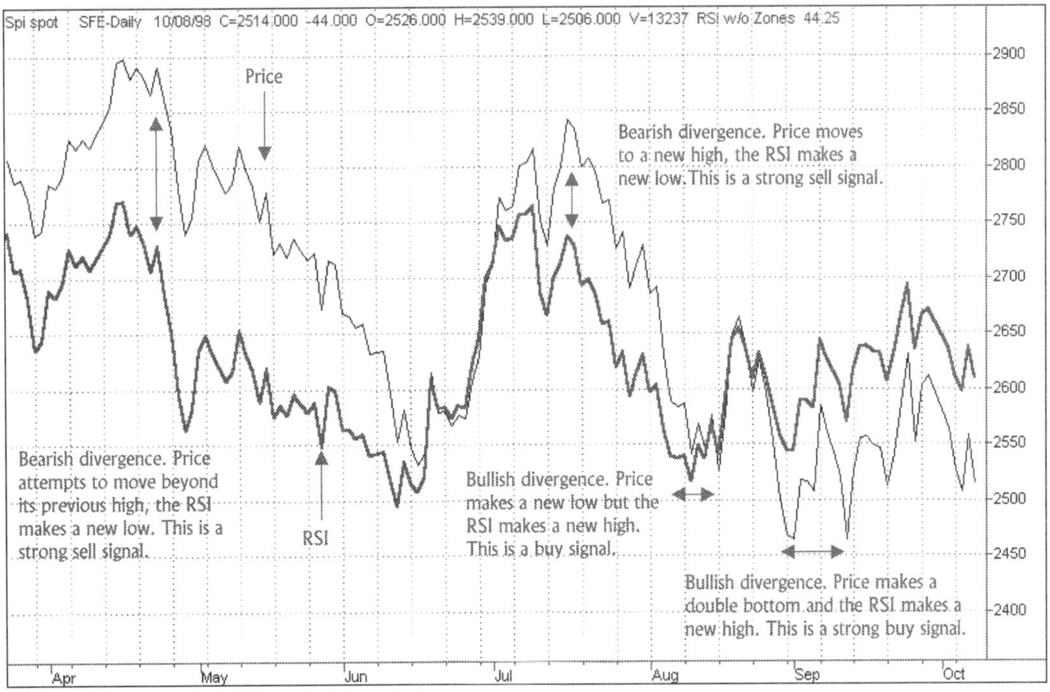

The second divergence is a more powerful example in that price does make a new high but the RSI makes a new low. This is a powerful signal. Traders are being warned by the market that there is a change coming. The astute trader would have seen this and rolled up any long positions and have been preparing to short the market. The resultant slippage saw the SPI lose approximately 300 points in a sustained downward move.

However, we must be aware that the divergence does not give us any clues as to the potential dimension of a move. Some divergences may be extremely strong and signal the beginning of a new sustained trend. Others may simply run out of energy after a few trading sessions.

The final point about divergence trading is not to be obsessed by looking for divergences. Strong divergences may only occur every few months, but that is more than sufficient to use them to aid you in your trading.

I have included a chart of NCP that has a number of divergences in it – see if you can spot them. The answers are in Appendix A.

FIG. 5.4 – NCP WITH RSI (1997)

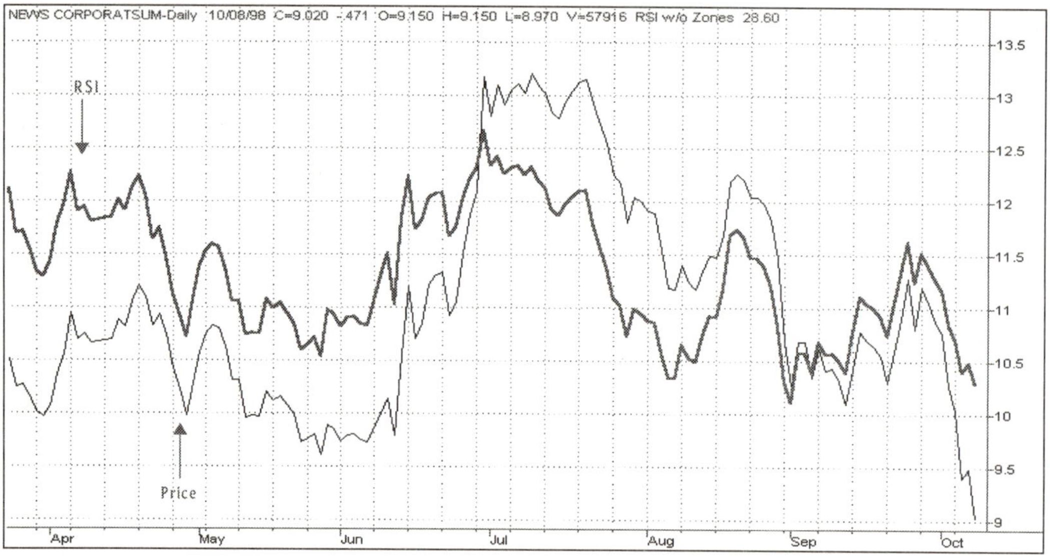

SRSI DIVERGENCES

The SRSI (Stochastic Relative Strength Index) is a variation on the traditional RSI in that it incorporates a stochastic function. In essence it is a hybrid indicator. It is not very widely used in Australia, and as a consequence is poorly understood and almost never incorporated into trading systems.

The SRSI actually takes the highest and lowest value for the original RSI and plugs this into the RSI equation. It does this for a number of values, so instead of merely calculating the RSI for, say, 13 days, as would occur in the traditional method, the SRSI takes the RSI for three time periods that the trader defines, calculates the highest and lowest RSI for these periods and then inserts these into the RSI equation.

The interpretation of the SRSI is much the same as for the RSI. We are looking for points where price and sentiment become dislocated. In the example of BHP (Fig. 5.5), there are two bearish divergences. These are points where price has moved to a new high but the SRSI has not been able to move beyond its previous high, thus confirming that the market has insufficient energy to continue in the direction of the established trend.

The SRSI also adds a secondary tool to our arsenal in that it highlights fatigue zones. These are the peaks and troughs of the SRSI. It can be seen that whenever the SRSI tracks to extreme values then price generally fatigues. It may or may not reverse with any degree of conviction, but it does slow. This slowing will provide the aggressive trader with opportunities for short, sharp trades. However, such a technique is only for the bold and the committed, because the SRSI can sit at an extreme value while prices continue to drift in the direction of the prevailing trend. Such a situation reminds us that we can only ever trade in the direction of the trend. What the SRSI does is alert us to potential changes in the trend so we can be ready.

FIG. 5.5 – BHP WITH SRSI

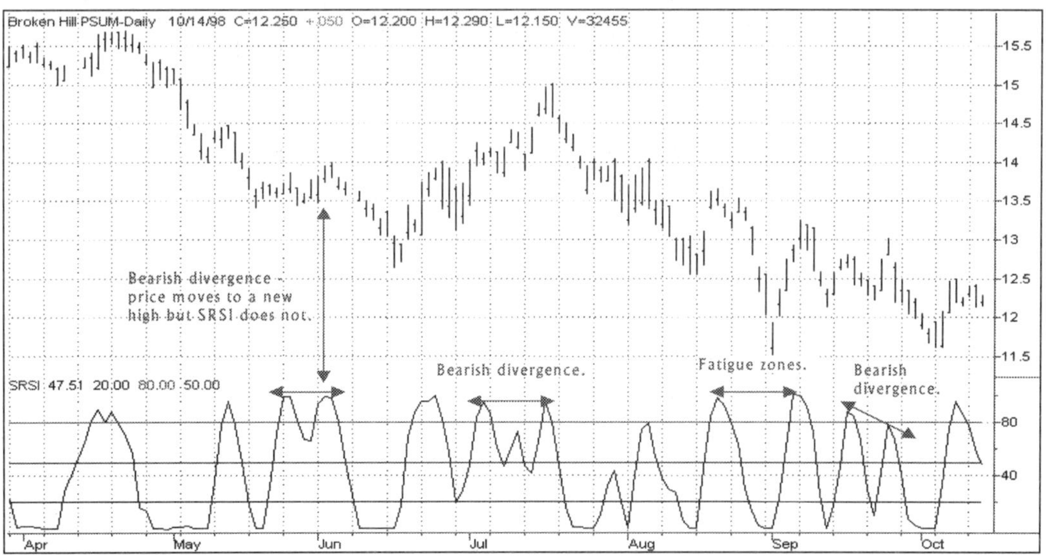

BREAK-OUT TRADING SYSTEMS

So far, in using tools to enable us to time our entry into the market, we have concentrated on trend analysis and divergence trading as separate entities. The break-out system I use draws these mechanisms into a single cohesive picture. However, the overwhelming criteria for this system – or any system for that matter – is the need for simplicity.

Trading systems that identify break-outs have been around for many decades – by definition any trend-following system will enable the trader to identify break-outs. The method I use for highlighting changes in sentiment was first popularised by Richard Donchian, a veteran technical analyst. This method was later adopted by Richard Dennis, a highly successful futures trader, and is the cornerstone of the methodology taught to the rather mysterious and secretive trading group known as the Turtles.

My application of the system revolves around three elements. First, I ask the charting package I use to highlight those days where the close for that particular day is either higher or lower than the preceding eight days. The computer then highlights these bars. In this text the downward breaks have a heavier definition – in the computer program they are given a different colour for ease of identification.

The second element in this system is the oscillator histogram known as Trend Power. This is a momentum-style indicator and it has several functions. Its prime functions are to keep the trader in the trend for as long as possible, identify divergence between price and sentiment, generate reversal or exit signals and to identify false signals that are sometimes generated by the break-out system. This final function is extremely important because all trading systems will give false signals, and it is essential that traders have some mechanism by which to sift through these signals.

"...all trading systems will give false signals, and it is essential that traders have some mechanism by which to sift through these signals."

The final component of the system is the SRSI. This indicator is a variation on the traditional RSI. The RSI was originally designed by J. Welles Wilder Jr, and its function is to measure changes in closing price. Therefore, the calculation of the RSI involves in part determining the average number of net up-closing days as a function of the average number of net down-closing days for the same period. This figure is then plugged into the traditional RSI calculation.

The interpretation of the SRSI is similar to that for the traditional RSI. The SRSI moves between a range of 0 to 100. Traders can then plot zones which, based upon historical observation and testing, pinpoint levels at which prices may be considered overbought or oversold. A more appropriate definition is that moves beyond the defined zones highlight areas where prices may fatigue and are prone to either stalling or slipping. The SRSI also highlights divergences between price and sentiment. Therefore, like the RSI, it is a coincident or leading indicator.

For the sake of convenience, I have broken the system into two parts. Initially I will only examine the histogram (Fig. 5.6). Since we are only interested in bearish trades, I have given the downtick bars of the system greater emphasis, so they can be easily delineated from the buy signals.

FIG. 5.6 – NCP WITH HISTOGRAM

In the above example of NCP, the effectiveness of this system in highlighting breaks in trend is evident. The rules for interpreting the system are simple. When given a sell signal, we stay short until we receive a reversal signal. This reversal signal is generally a slowing in the oscillator histogram. We will stay with a position as long as the histogram is trending in the same direction as price. When a divergence occurs we exit the trade.

In the period July to October 1998, the system gave three strong sell signals – the first in July, the second in August and the third in October. In each of these downward moves it can be seen how the histogram gave strong sell signals that persisted until a reversal signal was given. It should be noted that this system – like any other – is not the Holy Grail, it is merely a mechanical system designed to eliminate as much as possible any interference from the trader. The rules cannot be bent, nor can they be misinterpreted. When the system gives a sell signal, you sell. There is no other option.

However, a simple histogram by itself lacks to a degree the capacity to highlight divergences in price and sentiment. That is why it is essential to have both the oscillator histogram and the SRSI, which I use to spot divergences.

In the second NCP example (Fig. 5.7), the divergences are highlighted, showing their role in helping us spot bearish trading opportunities. You will note that the oscillator histogram has the capacity to identify divergences, as it does in late April. The SRSI identifies the major divergence before the large swing down in July. The identification of this divergence would also cause the trader to disregard the false buy signals that are given just before the move down in price. This system is also given added weight by the use of the SRSI in spotting divergence trades.

FIG. 5.7 – NCP WITH BREAK-OUT SYSTEM

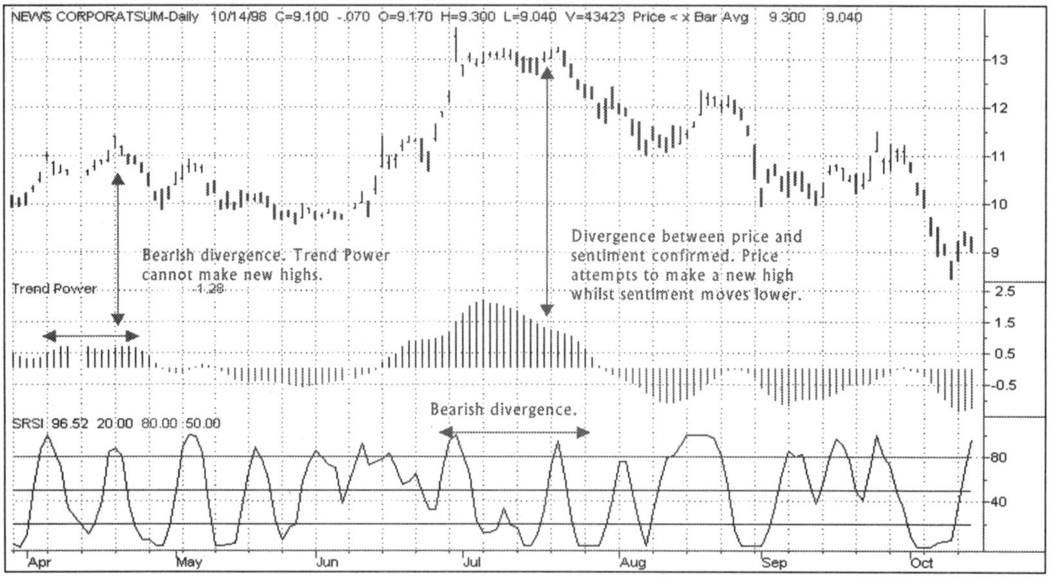

CONCLUSION

Much is written about designing trading systems. In my opinion, too much is written about trading system design, since in actuality it is the least important part of trading. Psychology and money management are far more important, yet they receive the least attention. The reasons for this are obvious. It is easy to write about moving averages, oscillators, divergences and the like. Browse through any book store and you will see literally hundreds of texts, all of which repeat themselves over and over and none of which bring anything new to the field of system design. System design and sales are also very lucrative – software companies make hundreds of millions of dollars flogging their wares. I am not saying that you do not need to use software – you do, because it gives you a means of interpreting price action. What I am saying is that there are no magic systems. Some work and some don't, but none will ever guarantee you fame, wealth, happiness and a smaller waistline.

I have attempted to communicate the fact that system design is a relatively easy process, involving only a few indicators. From personal experience I can testify that it is easy to be seduced by the battery of indicators that are present in systems. The system I use now (SuperCharts) is a middle-of-the-road package. It comes with about 80 native indicators. I could go to the SuperCharts download site and download probably a further 200, yet none of these indicators would add to my profitability, nor would any be superior to the system I already use. The quest in system design should not be to use more and more indicators but to use less and less. System design is like sculpting a block of marble – you chip away until you achieve the desired result. You never see sculptors adding to their blocks of marble.

"System design is like sculpting a block of marble – you chip away until you achieve the desired result."

6: INDEX TRADING

IN THIS AND the following chapter we will look at the tools available to bears for trading markets that have rapid breakdowns in price, and markets that are consolidating or moving sideways. These tools are futures and options. It is necessary for traders to understand that markets spend less than 20% of their time actually trending, so if your trading techniques are reliant upon trending markets you will spend a lot of time twiddling your thumbs as prices consolidate.

THE SPI

The Share Price Index (SPI) is a futures contract over the All Ordinaries Index, hence moves in the All Ordinaries are accompanied by moves in the SPI. This relationship can be seen in the charts on the following page.

We can see that if the index is flat then the SPI is flat. If the index is trending down then the SPI is trending down. We therefore have an instrument for trading the broader market. However, it is important to note, before we look at trading the SPI, that futures contracts must trend in order for us to be profitable, hence we need direction. If the SPI remains flat, then we are merely marking time. It is also important that you understand the fundamentals of futures trading before you attempt to trade the SPI. Futures contracts are highly leveraged instruments, and can cause serious financial difficulty for the unwary. If you do not know what a futures contract is, you might want to read *Understanding Futures Trading in Australia* (Wrightbooks, 1998), or get in touch with the Sydney Futures Exchange about attending one of their introductory courses. If you attempt to trade futures without any preparation whatsoever, you are committing financial suicide.

On page 69 the contract specifications of the SPI are given. Each contract has a dollar value that is equal to 25 times the value of the All Ordinaries Index. For example, if the AOI is at 2500 points, the dollar value of the contract is $62,500. Each point the SPI contract moves is worth $25, and you can trade contracts in any of the quarterly settlement months, up until the last business day of the actual contract month.

FIG. 6.1 – ALL ORDINARIES INDEX (1998)

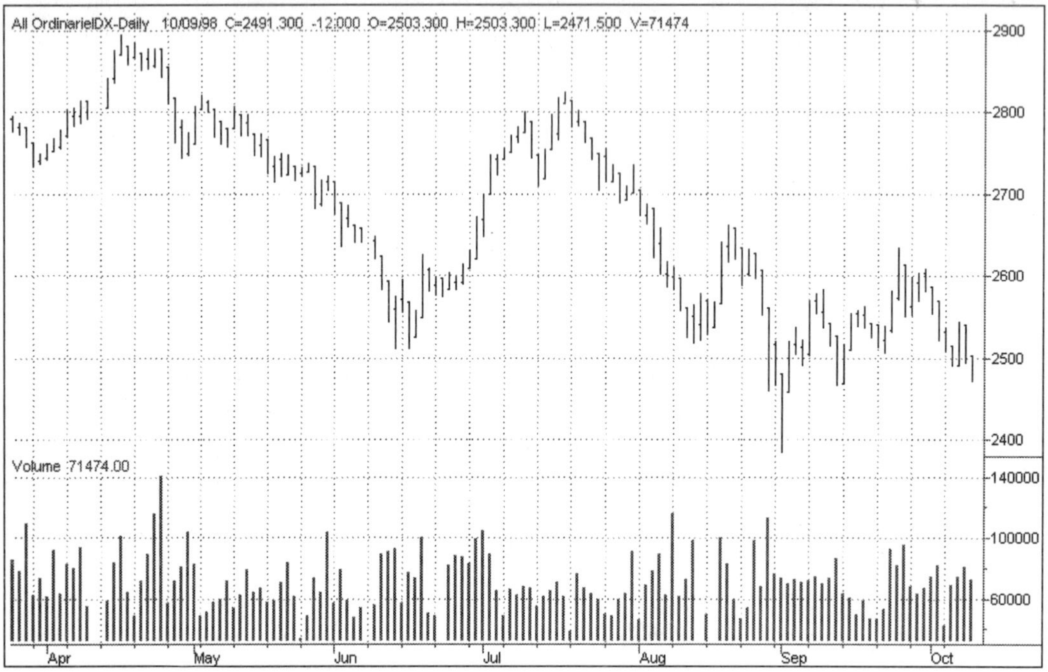

FIG. 6.2 – SHARE PRICE INDEX (1998)

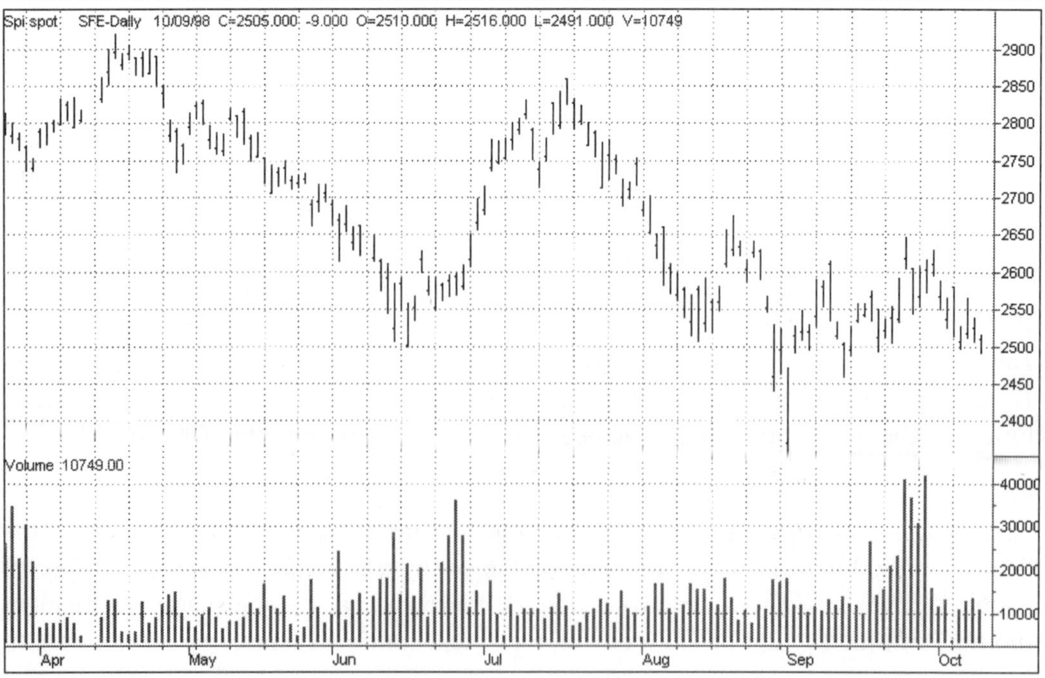

SPI CONTRACT SPECIFICATIONS

Contract Unit:	A sum of money equal to 25 times the All Ordinaries Index, expressed in Australian dollars.
Price Quotation:	The price is expressed in the same terms as the All Ordinaries Index, expressed to one full point. The minimum fluctuation of 1.0 point is equal to $25.00 per futures contract.
Settlement Price:	The closing quotation for the All Ordinaries Index on the last day of trading calculated to one decimal point, as adjusted and provided by the Australian Stock Exchange.
Cash Settlement:	All bought and sold contracts in existence as at the close of trade shall be settled by the Clearing House at the cash settlement price.
Contract Months:	March, June, September and December up to 18 months in advance.
Termination of Trading:	The last business day of the contract month, trading ceases at 4.10 p.m.
Settlement Day:	The second-last business day following the last permitted day of trading.
Trading Hours:	Floor: 9.30 a.m. - 12.30 p.m./2.00 p.m. - 4.10 p.m. SYCOM: 4.40 p.m. - 6.00 a.m.

BEAR TRADING THE SPI

Before beginning our exploration of trading the SPI, it is necessary to reinforce an essential point: to trade the SPI successfully we need it to trend. The direction of the trend is irrelevant, we just need it to trend. It is impossible to trade the SPI directly when it is moving in a sideways direction.

In trading the SPI from the short side, we need to follow many of the analytical pathways that were illustrated earlier: we need to have some means of viewing the SPI and deciding whether or not it is trending down. Such a methodology is dependent upon us defining the trend.

FIG. 6.3 – SHARE PRICE INDEX

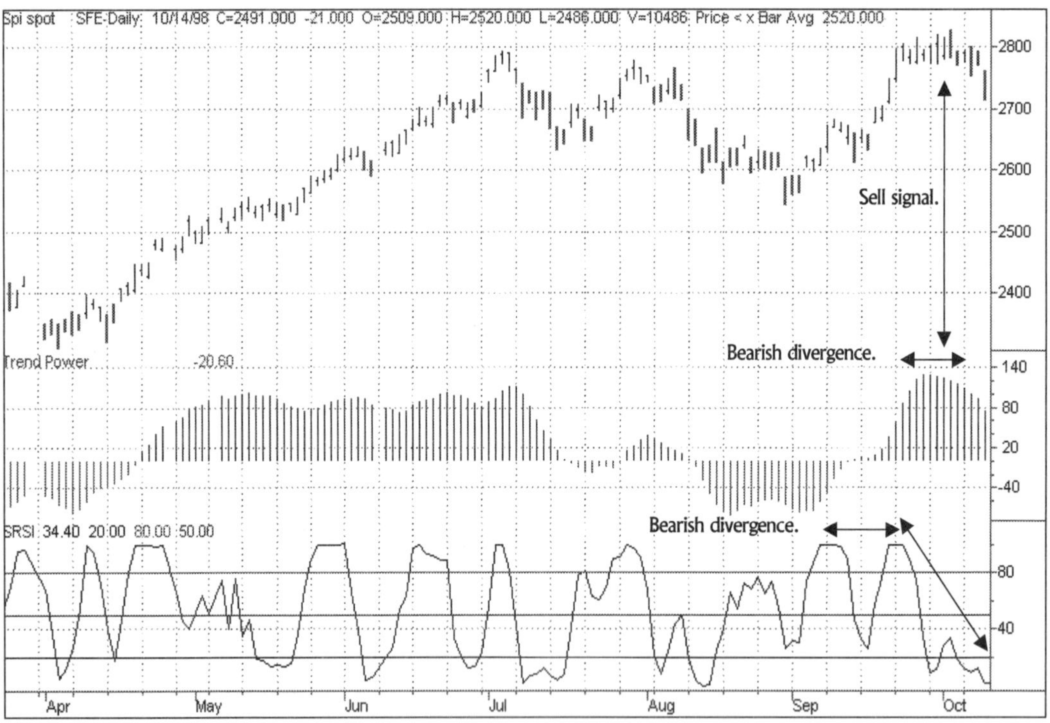

The above chart is of the SPI in the period prior to the breakdown in October 1997. This period illustrates how prices can swing from bullish to bearish very quickly. The indicators applied here are from the break-out system that was introduced in the previous chapter.

In the four weeks leading up to the perturbation in October, the market had been in a clearly defined uptrend, and all traders should have been pointing in this direction.

The market then began to consolidate around the 2800 mark. This consolidation was a sign to scale back long positions because the market seemed to have difficulty moving ahead. Prices consistently retreated from the low 2800 region.

We have established a body of evidence that shows the market was struggling to go higher, and that our primary trend indicators were calling the market down. Our instruction to our broker would therefore have been to sell the SPI once it had broken through our primary trend indicator during October 1997. Thus we would have been short the SPI from approximately 2770. Notice that we are not expecting a crash – that word should never enter our vocabulary. We are merely expecting a retracement in prices.

However, we would not have exited the position, even after the initial move down, because our downtrend was still in place. Trends persist and should be followed until they reverse. You will never make much money jumping on and off trends before they reach some form of climax. Just as we use trend-following indicators to initiate a trade, then likewise we should use trend-following indicators to define when we exit a trade (Fig 6.4).

FIG. 6.4 – SPI EXIT SIGNAL

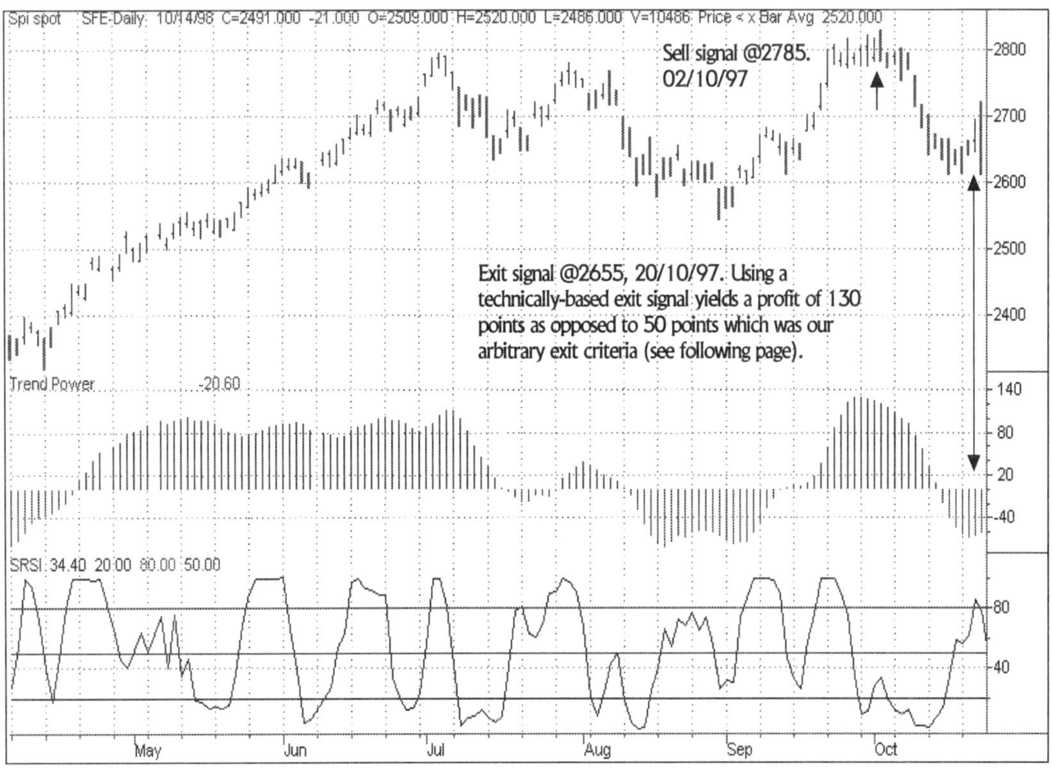

The acceleration of this move was unexpected. However, it is time for one of those irritating reality checks – trading a trending market is quite easy. Using trend-following indicators to trade the SPI is not brain surgery. Strong discipline should keep you from making tragic mistakes and you should always be on the right side of the market. The difficulty arises when you attempt to trade markets that are choppy.

TRADING RULE

Wait for confirmation before entering a trade. Your primary trend indicator must confirm the direction of the market. This indicator should not be overridden by other indicators, wishful thinking or your own psychological bias.

EXIT RULES

The discussion so far has focused only on when to initiate a trade. This is only half of the story. If you do not get your exit right, you will not make any money. We have seen that trends persist, and should be followed until they reverse. Adopting this strategy involves a slight bending of one of the prime rules of trading. In virtually every trading book you pick up, you will be told that it is necessary to set profit targets before initiating a trade. There is, however, a problem with this approach. You will have no idea at what point a trend will end, and no idea how far a trend will go or at what price-level the move will be exhausted. To set profit targets before a trade has been set in place implies that you know how far particular prices will go – a remarkable psychic ability. Unfortunately, this is impossible, and to set profit targets beforehand is to initiate a negative mental strategy because you are going to take money off the table pre-emptively. To illustrate this point we need to return to our SPI trade.

Assume that before we initiate our trade, we set our profit target at 50 points (this is an arbitrary figure used just for this example). We have entered the trade at 2785 and have decided to exit at 2735 (Fig. 6.4). (If we refer back to our chart of the SPI, we can see that in October 1997 our sell signal was given at 2785. I have assumed that we shorted the market at the low for this particular day.) If we assume that we trade three contracts, our maximum profit would be 3 × 25 × 50 =$3,750. Not a bad return for a few days.

"If you do not get your exit right, you will not make any money."

However, let's assume that we had decided to use a technically-based exit system (Fig. 6.5), i.e. we only reverse when we get an exit signal in the form of an uptick bar. This will indicate a change in trend.

Our signal to exit comes on October 20, at 2655. If we had let our trade run until then, our initial profit would have been 3 × 25 × 130 = $9,750.

Obeying our technically-based system, we would have then reversed and initiated a long-side trade at 2655. We cannot tell the future, we can only obey the rules of our system. A close-up of the period shows how we would have exited our short position on October 20, and initiated a long position that was again reversed on October 22 at 2656. The latest the position should have been reversed was October 23 at 2637. To be conservative, we will assume that the reversal was late, and we took a loss of 18 points on the long-side trade (2655 – 2637 = 18), and we are again short from 2637.

FIG. 6.5 – SPI REVERSAL SIGNAL

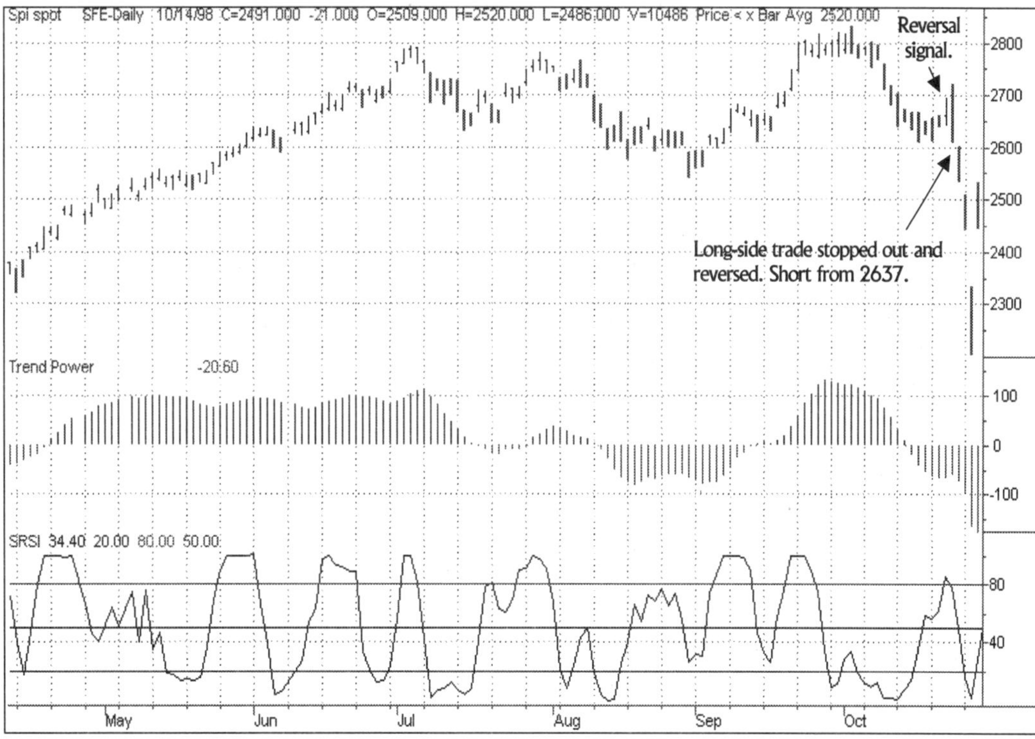

It is at this time that we have to introduce both a level of flexibility and an understanding of how the market works. Many traders, when they enter a position, assume that dramatic and forceful moves will continue forever in a given direction. To use an expression from my high school physics classes, prices are not infinitely elastic: they rebound after forceful moves.

FIG. 6.6 – SPI CORRECTION

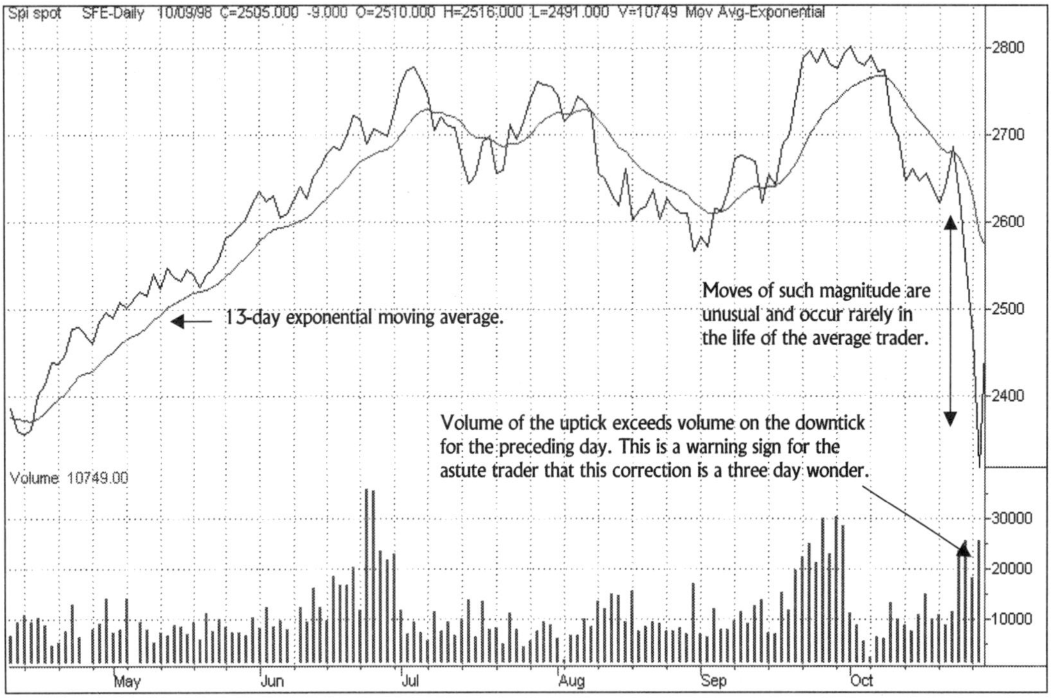

You will notice in the chart of the actual correction (Fig. 6.6) the rather obvious notation of it being an unusual market event. This is not a facetious remark, rather one that has enormous statistical validity. If you look at the above chart, you will notice how the moving average and price run almost parallel. When price moves too far away from the moving average, it eventually rebounds back toward the average. This regression means that short-side traders must be ready for these bounces back toward the average, and use them to capture some of the profit built into a trade. However, it is difficult to do, and requires a degree of blind faith in what you are doing. It is also quite imprecise, and the astute reader will have realised that it breaches our rule of following a trend until a technical liquidation signal is given.

In the above chart, there is a clue as to the strength of the bounce that followed the initial correction to be found in the volume in the market. If you look at the extreme right-hand edge of the chart, you will see that volume on the bounce up actually exceeds volume on the preceding down-day. This is an early warning signal. As we saw in our history lesson about crashes, there is no follow-through volume on up-days. If October 1997 had been a true crash, uptick volume would have been dramatically smaller than downtick volume. However, much of this is seen with the luxury of hindsight. It is extremely difficult to be aware of all these things during periods of explosive moves.

If we return to our initial short trade, and use only our criterion of a clear reversal signal from the break-out system, we can see how the trade would be resolved.

Our exit signal was given on November 3 at 2505, so our profit on the trade would have been 3 × 25 × 150 = $11,250. For argument's sake, let's assume that we got lucky and sold at the low of 2210. Our profit would have been 3 × 25 × 427 = $32,025. To hit the low would have been unbelievably lucky – the chances of actually doing so would have been close to zero. In such a market, a prudent trader would have scaled out of the position by taking profits on the way down. Again, this does seem like a breach of our trading rules, however such markets are extraordinarily unusual and they require unusual techniques. Remember your first rule should be to ensure your survival, your second rule should be to make a profit. This is especially true in a volatile market.

7: USING OPTIONS TO TRADE THE SPI

DIRECTLY TRADING THE SPI is not the only method available to bears who want to trade the index: options are also traded over the SPI. I will touch only briefly on the mechanics of options. If you are unfamiliar with exchange-traded options, I suggest you read *Understanding Options Trading in Australia* (Wrightbooks, 1997) and/or do one of the courses on options that are run by ASX Derivatives.

Exchange-traded options come in two types: calls and puts. A call option gives the holder of the option the right, but not the obligation, to buy the underlying futures contract according to the terms of the option. A put option gives the holder of the option the right, but not the obligation, to sell the underlying futures contract. The four basic option strategies are outlined below. All other strategies are built up from these four strategies.

For the sake of this text, we are only interested in those strategies that have a bearish tone, so we are only interested in either buying puts or selling calls over the SPI.

STRATEGY	RISK	EXPECTED MOVE
Buy a call option	Limited to the premium paid	*Bullish* – Potential profit unlimited
Sell a call option	Unlimited risk	*Bearish* – Profit limited to premium
Buy a put option	Limited to the premium paid	*Bearish* – Potential profit unlimited
Sell a put option	Unlimited risk	*Bullish* – Profit limited to premium

Buying Put Options

Put options can be bearish instruments. They allow the buyer of the put the right, but not the obligation, to sell the SPI at a set level by a predetermined expiry date. If we return to the period of October 1997 (previous chapter), instead of selling the SPI as our initial trade, we could have bought a put option.

Put options have strike prices 25 points apart so, based upon our initial example in which we received a sell signal at 2770, we would have bought a put option with a strike price of either 2775 or 2750, with an expiry in December.

"...the majority of traders do not understand the concept of risk/reward."

It is here that I have to introduce a note of caution: most option trades fail. They fail for a variety of reasons, such as traders having no trading method, so they make a guess about market direction. They also fail because the majority of traders do not understand the concept of risk/reward. When faced with an opportunity, the majority of traders want the magic windfall that will make them rich overnight. This *never* happens – remember the first rule of trading is survival, not making money. In choosing what option to buy, we apply the same logic. We do not know how far any given move will go, so we are naturally prudent. Poor traders, instead of buying options that are at or near the money, will buy very cheap options that are well out-of-the-money. Such a strategy is doomed to failure.

Assume that we have two separate trades running, and that we have bought the Dec 2775 puts for 35 and the Dec 2750 puts for 25. At expiry, we have a range of possible outcomes for our first trade (Table 7.1). These are shown in the following payoff diagram.

DECEMBER 2775 PUTS

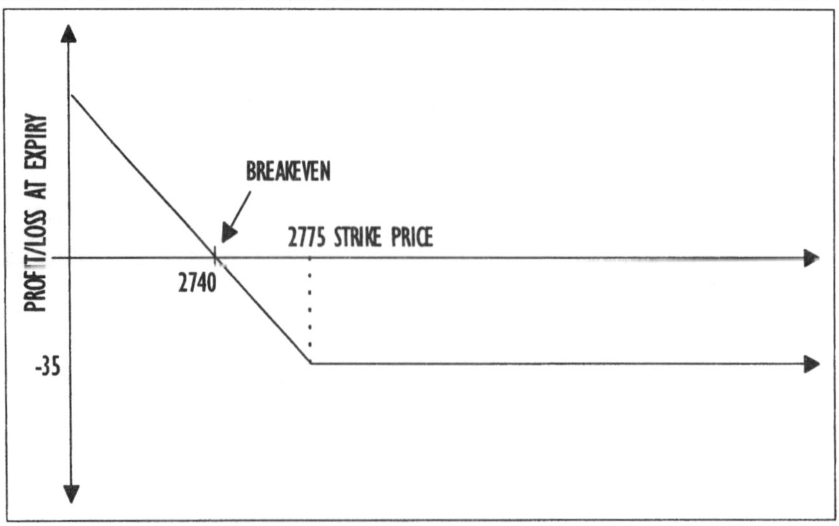

TABLE 7.1 – DECEMBER 2775 PUTS

PRICE AT EXPIRY	OPTION PRICE	PROFIT/LOSS
2775	0	-35
2760	15	-20
2750	25	-10
2740	35	breakeven
2730	45	10
2720	55	20
2710	65	30
2700	75	40
2690	85	50
2680	95	60
2670	105	70
2660	115	80
2650	125	90
2640	135	100
2630	145	110
2620	155	120
2610	165	130
2600	175	140

A similar range of scenarios can be generated for the Dec 2750 puts (payoff diagram below and Table 7.2 on following page).

DECEMBER 2750 PUTS

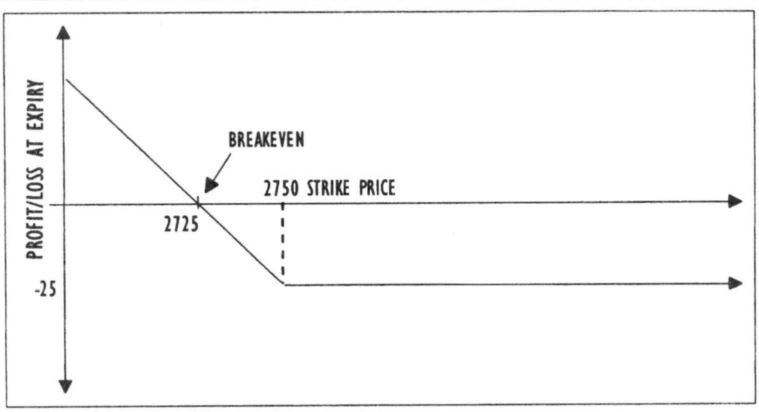

TABLE 7.2 – DECEMBER 2750 PUTS

PRICE AT EXPIRY	OPTION PRICE	PROFIT/LOSS
2770	0	-25
2760	0	-25
2750	0	-25
2740	10	-15
2730	20	-5
2720	30	5
2710	40	15
2700	50	25
2690	60	35
2680	70	45
2670	80	55
2660	90	65
2650	100	75
2640	110	85
2630	120	95
2620	130	105
2610	140	115
2600	150	125

What is immediately apparent from these two tables is that our at-the-money put (Dec 2775) has a wider range over which it is profitable. The Dec 2750 position, because it is out-of-the-money, requires a larger downward move to be profitable. However, this is only part of the story, and does not reflect the relative leverage of the two positions. Let's assume that we had taken both positions at the time of receiving our initial sell signal at 2770, and that we exited the position upon receiving our buy signal at 2660. Assume that the options are selling for purely intrinsic value, and that there is no time component left nor any speculative premium built into the price.

"What is immediately apparent from these two tables is that our at-the-money put (Dec 2775) has a wider range over which it is profitable."

Dec 2775 put = 109 points (74 points profit) = 211% return

Dec 2750 put = 84 points (59 points profit) = 236% return

As we would expect, the cheaper option offers greater leverage for a given move in price. However, that leverage is dependent upon price moving with sufficient velocity to make the option profitable. This brings us to the concept of risk/reward, and a bit of old Wall Street philosophy: *there are old traders and there are bold traders, but there are no old bold traders.*

The point is that the first rule of trading is survival. If you go around buying out-of-the-money options hoping for the one big score, you will not survive. Your options trading should revolve around the principle of buying at-the-money options. Never buy deep out-of-the-money options – unless you get a very big move they will be worthless.

> *TRADING RULE*
> ***Trade to survive, not to make money.*** If you survive, the money will come.

Selling Call Options

If we refer back to our earlier definition, you will remember that buying a call option is a bullish strategy. Buying a call option confers upon the holder the right, but not the obligation, to buy the underlying futures contract by a set expiry date at a set strike price. The extension of this is that the writer of the call option is, by definition, bearish in outlook, and is hoping to profit by a decrease in the value of the option. The writer of a call option is, in essence, a short-seller. They have sold the option to the buyer at a given price, and they want the price of the underlying contract to decrease so that the option decreases in value. The writer has two choices: buy the option back and pocket the profit, or, if the move is sustained, let it expire.

As bears, we are interested in selling calls to take advantage of any movement down in the underlying SPI contract. The mechanics of this are illustrated in the following example.

The sell signals that give us confidence to either short the SPI or buy put options are identical to the signals to sell or write calls. If we apply a simple break-out system, we can see the types of call-selling opportunities that occur in the chart on the following page (Fig. 7.1).

FIG. 7.1 – SHARE PRICE INDEX

We can identify a clear sell signal in the first week of May. Let's assume that we take this signal and sell the June 2800 call for 20 points. A range of outcomes is possible.

TABLE 7.3 – JUNE 2800 CALLS

PRICE AT EXPIRY	OPTION PRICE	PROFIT/LOSS
2870	*70*	*-50*
2860	*60*	*-40*
2850	*50*	*-30*
2840	*40*	*-20*
2830	*30*	*-10*
2820	*20*	*breakeven*
2810	*10*	*10*
2800	*0*	*20*
2790	*0*	*20*
2780	*0*	*20*
2770	*0*	*20*
2760	*0*	*20*

JUNE 2800 CALLS

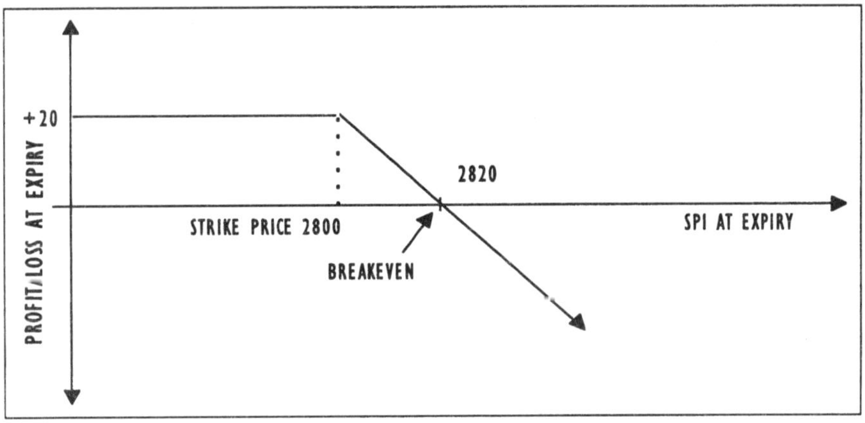

As can be seen from our range of possible outcomes, the profit on the trade is limited to the initial premium received from selling the call option. We can never make any more on the trade than this amount. Conversely, the risk on this particular trade is theoretically unlimited. If the SPI, at the expiration of the options contract, is above the breakeven point of 2820, losses will be incurred. It is important that this point be understood and burned into your psyche, otherwise you are likely to suffer a catastrophic loss. In short-selling options, your profit is limited to your initial premium. Your loss is theoretically unlimited.

RANGE-TRADING TECHNIQUES FOR THE SPI

As we have said before, as bears we are interested not only in markets that are trending down, but also markets that are moving sideways. Range-trading markets call for specialist techniques. These techniques should not be attempted by the novice.

The first point to note is that you cannot directly trade the SPI in a market that is moving sideways. Many people will try and tell you that it is possible to trade the small whipsaws that occur in price action when a market is moving sideways. The same people will probably tell you that Elvis visits their local 7-11 every Friday night. Attempting to trade whipsaws is a pointless activity. I have never met anybody who has been able to do it successfully. The prime rule in trading is to trade the prevailing trend: if the trend is up you go long, if the trend is down you go short, and if the trend is sideways you use tactics that have been devised to take into account sideways movement in the market.

However, before even beginning to think about trading a consolidating market, you need to be able to identify consolidation patterns in the market. Earlier in this book, we looked at the broad phases of the market, and these broad phases apply equally well to the SPI. They are far too imprecise and vague, though, to base trading decisions upon. Trading decisions must be based upon more refined techniques.

When we looked at plotting trendlines, I mentioned that it was essential to get into the habit of plotting a return line. As we begin to explore the trading of congestion patterns, the reason for this will become apparent. Without a return line, we cannot define a congestion zone – if we cannot define the congestion zone then we will not know when prices have broken away from the zone, hence we will be flying blind in an extremely unstable area of the market. It is essential to remember that prices break explosively out of congestion zones. Without clearly defined criteria our chances of suffering a catastrophic loss are high.

FIG. 7.2 – SHARE PRICE INDEX (1998)

Fig. 7.2 concentrates on the period of mid-September 1997 to mid-October 1997. It shows the SPI trading in a range of approximately 26 points, based upon the close. Intra-day trading took the SPI slightly outside this range, but based upon closing prices, a low of 2777 and a high of 2803 had been established for this three week period. We have established a range of values within which traders seem comfortable to trade the SPI. There was insufficient impetus to push prices beyond these limits during this time frame. It is this sort of movement that the bear who wants to trade choppy markets is looking for.

It can also be seen that volatility for that particular period was both low and constant. Such an indicator merely confirms that prices are range trading.

The Written Straddle

The techniques for trading a consolidating SPI are options-based, and they are generated by selling or writing both puts and calls. The first technique we will look at is the written straddle. The written straddle involves selling or writing both a put and a call option with identical terms, i.e. strike price and expiry date.

Let's assume that we have performed the above analysis. We know that the market is range-trading and we wish to take advantage of this.

To do this, we sell the Dec 2800 call and put for 25 and 30 points respectively. We have therefore received 55 points in premium income. The objective of the strategy is to take advantage of the sideways movement in the SPI, and allow time-decay to diminish the value of the options so that they can be bought back at a lower price. A secondary objective of the trade is that, if the SPI breaks in a given direction, the leg that is in-the-money and generating a loss will be closed out and the profitable leg left to run (note that in generating a written straddle, one leg will always be in-the-money). This trade will be profitable if the SPI, at expiry of the put, is somewhere between 2855 and 2745.

WRITTEN STRADDLE

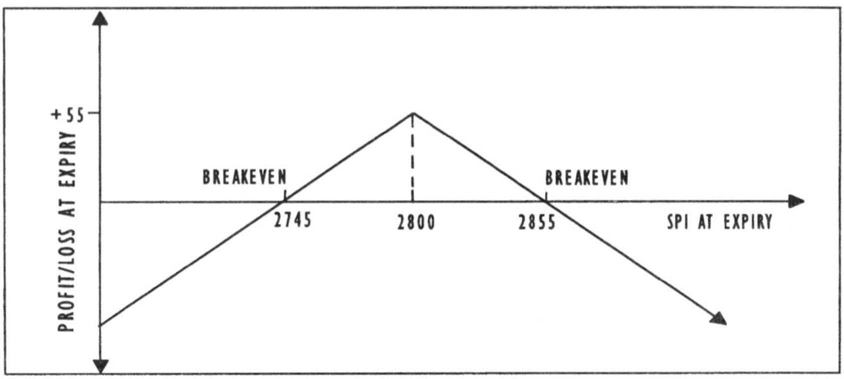

This outcome is based upon the assumption that the trade is left untouched until expiry. This is an unlikely occurrence. If we refer back to our charts of the SPI (Fig. 6.2 and Fig. 6.3), in which the trading range was defined, it can be seen that the SPI exploded out of the trading range. In such a situation, there is the possibility of taking a heavy loss very quickly. The longer a trading range is in force, the more explosive will be the move out of the trading range. It is best to think of a trading range as a spring that is being wound tighter and tighter as time passes. When the spring is released, the move – in whatever direction it comes – has a great deal of energy behind it. Such a situation is evidenced by the rapid movement in the SPI at the time of the October correction. If this trade had been left untouched, the loss that would have been incurred would have been of the order of several hundred points.

> **"The written straddle is a specialist trading technique that is suited to drifting markets."**

The written straddle is a specialist trading technique that is suited to drifting markets. It can only be utilised with rigid risk management, and it can only be used by experienced option traders, because, in a trending market, it is possible for the market to move beyond the zone of profitability very quickly. Do not apply this technique and think that the relatively large premium you generate will protect you – in a trending market it will not.

The Written Strangle

The written strangle is constructed by selling calls and puts that have identical expiry dates but differing strike prices. If a written strangle was constructed during the time of the SPI's consolidation in September/October, it would be constructed by selling the Dec 2825 call and the Dec 2775 put. Let's assume that this has been done, and that 35 points of premium has been generated. The profitability zone for such a trade is 2860 to 2740, a range of 120 points. This strategy is more profitable over a wider range of outcomes than the written straddle.

WRITTEN STRANGLE

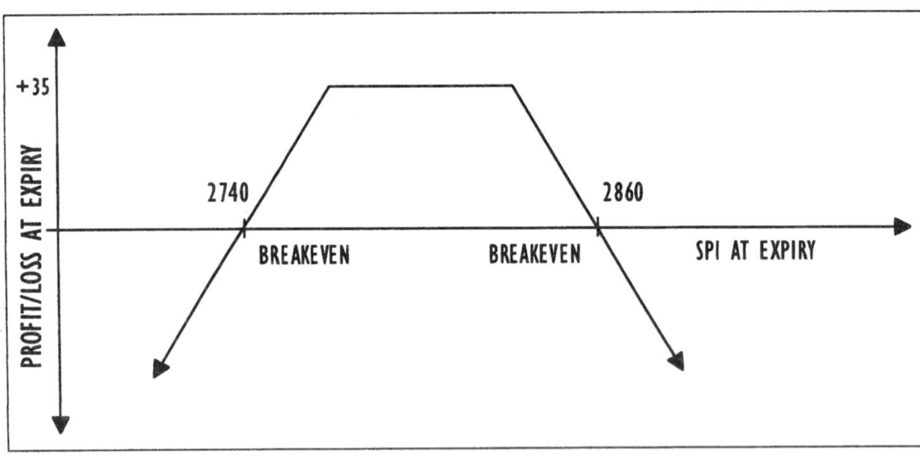

However, like all written strategies, the maximum profit that can be achieved is the initial premium. We can never make any more than that, yet our maximum loss is theoretically unlimited.

A Final Word About Trading Choppy Markets

Choppy or range-trading markets are a grey area in a market's development. It is impossible to predict in what direction the market will break. As can be seen by any of the previous charts of the SPI, when the market does break it does so with a great deal of ferocity. It can leave you confused and anxious. The worst scenario is that you will freeze under the stress of a rapidly moving market, thereby guaranteeing a catastrophic loss.

If you wish to trade the congestion area that markets sometimes enter, do your homework, establish what the true range is and use that to define your exit points. If you have not done one of the SFE's courses on futures trading, or if you have not read and understood *Understanding Futures Trading in Australia* or a similar book, do not even contemplate trading the SPI or its options.

8: PORTFOLIO MANAGEMENT FOR BEAR MARKETS

THERE ARE A variety of market participants who, for reasons of their own, shun the use of derivatives such as options and futures, and quasi-derivatives such as warrants. Such an attitude minimises the range of tactical alternatives that they can employ in a bear market. However, it does leave one staggeringly obvious technique for surviving a bear market – *sell*. Do not average down, do not buy dips, do not engage in dollar-cost averaging and do not be swayed by the nonsense that you are insulated by your dividends or any other intellectually bankrupt idea. If your shares are going down, sell the damned things. If you were on a train that was going in the wrong direction, you would get off at the earliest opportunity, not wait for it to reach its destination, where you have to get off again and wait for a train that was going in your direction to come along and collect you – yet this is precisely what the majority of market participants do. The only time to own shares is when they are going *up*, not when they are going *down*. The chart below shows what happens to the passive investor.

"One should buy good stocks that go up and if they don't go up, don't buy them."

WILL ROGERS

FIG. 8.1 – MIM HOLDINGS (1998)

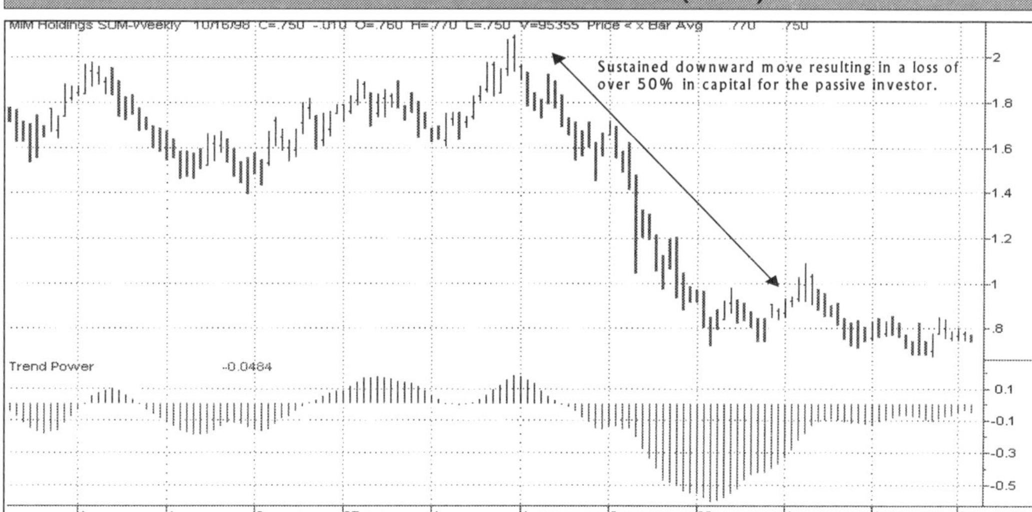

RULES FOR PORTFOLIO TRADING

The rules for portfolio trading are strikingly simple: when you receive a sell signal, you *sell*. You do not engage in any of the following:

1. Averaging down – buying more of something that is going down is a fool's exercise.
2. Dollar-cost averaging – this is fund manager talk for averaging down. Just because someone is paid $250,000 to make decisions for you does not make it any less stupid than averaging down.
3. Buying dips – if it is going down, it is going down. A slight slowing is irrelevant.
4. Being convinced that you are insulated by your dividends – consider the following example: based upon your broker's advice, you buy BHP at $20, only to see it fall to $12. You have just lost 40% of your investment. When you complain about this, your broker says that you are protected by your dividend. At a dividend rate of 3.5% per annum, theoretically you will get your initial investment back in a little over 11 years. In reality, you will never recover because you run into concepts such as the real cost of money and opportunity cost. You never buy or hold a share because of its dividend. You only buy things you think are going up.
5. Be calmed by the belief that good stocks always recover – if you believe this, consider the fate of David Jones Ltd, Qintex and Bell Group. All were once considered good stocks. Consider the charts of Amcor and WMC (opposite). Both of these (at the time of writing) had been in prolonged bear markets, and will need exceptional growth to recover.
6. Believe that brokerage and taxation are relevant – they are both irrelevant. Portfolios today can be liquidated for a fraction of the cost that was previously possible, and I would rather share a $100,000 profit with the tax man than keep a $50,000 loss to myself.

Short-Selling

The passive technique of simply exiting the market once a sell signal has been given allows portfolio traders to preserve their capital, but it does not allow them to be profitable, since, having withdrawn from the market, they have to look for trading opportunities outside the equities market. As we all know, taking your money out of a declining market is prudent and eminently sensible, but it incurs an opportunity cost of not being able to profit from the decline in the value of shares. The ability to short-sell shares offers the portfolio trader the chance to profit from declines in the market. Consider the example of Crown Casino (Fig. 8.4, page 92).

"The ability to short-sell shares offers the portfolio trader the chance to profit from declines in the market."

FIG. 8.2 – AMCOR

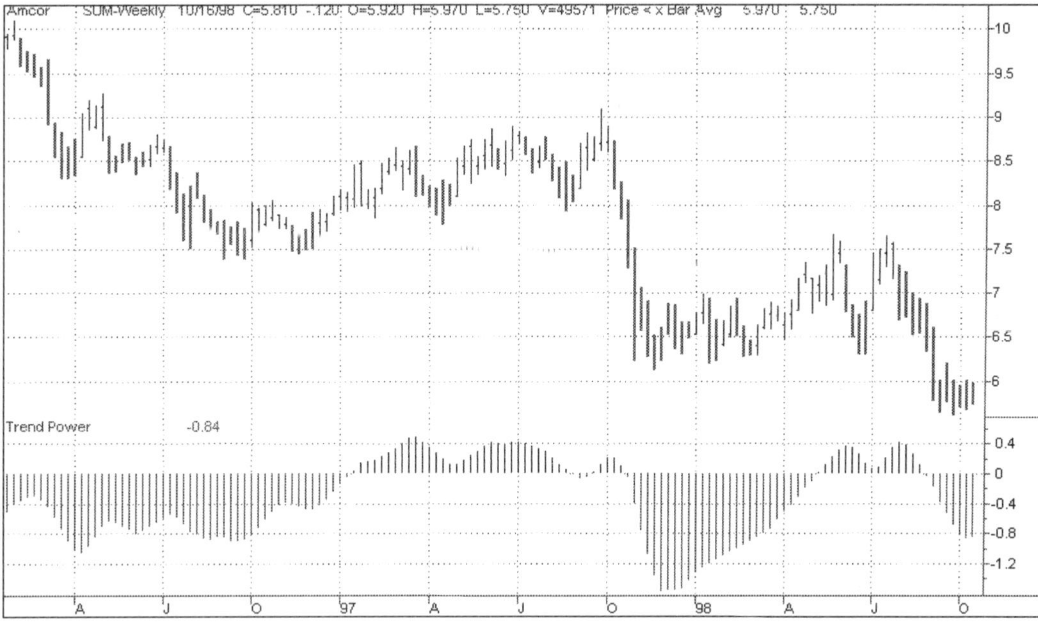

FIG. 8.3 – WESTERN MINING

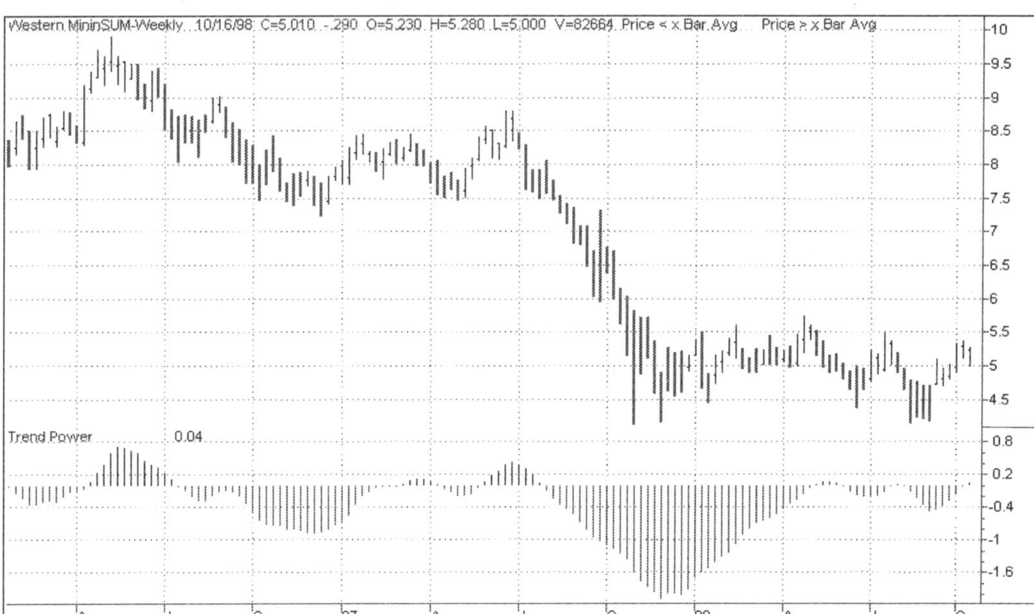

FIG. 8.4 – CROWN CASINO SELL SIGNALS (1997)

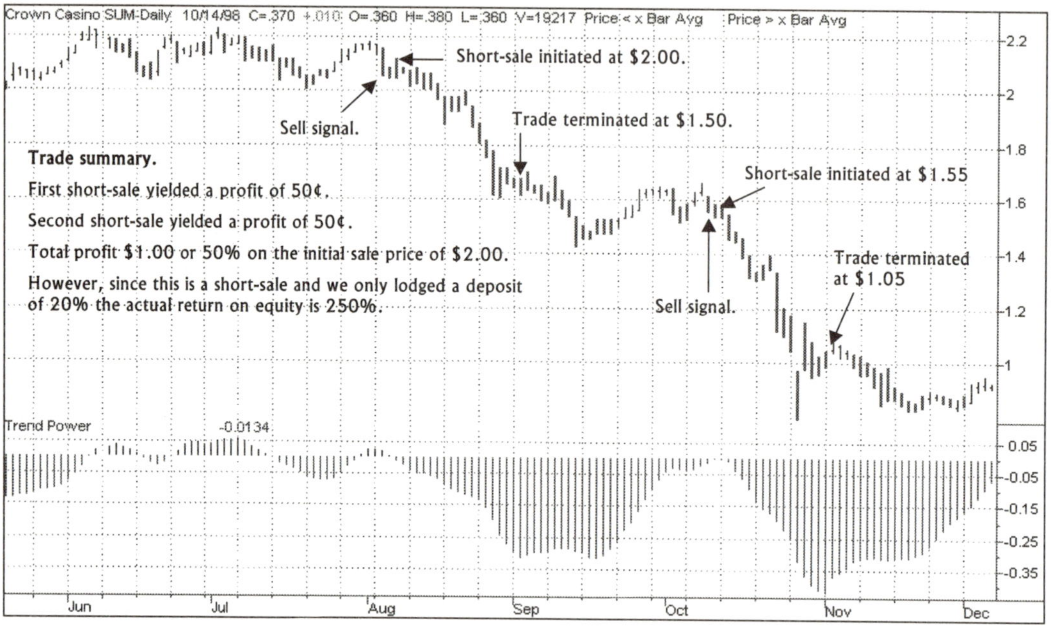

I have chosen Crown Casino to illustrate short-selling for a variety of reasons. First, it listed during a bull market. As such, you would expect it to have considerable general market momentum. Secondly, its listing was accompanied by a great deal of hype and positive expectation. Investors were soothed by statements such as "Casinos never go broke", "Good stocks always go up", etc., etc. As a consequence of this, those who owned Crown shares had a great deal of emotional attachment to the stock. By the end of this section, you should see the folly of being emotionally attached to a share or being seduced by any of the nonsense you hear.

In this example, we can see a daily chart of the price-action of Crown Casino. This chart shows our entry and exit points for short-sale opportunities in the price history of Crown Casino. The trade is exited when a reversal signal is given.

Before looking at the mechanics of how this trading technique works and its potential profitability, it is necessary to define exactly what short-selling is. Short-selling is the technique by which you short-sell a stock which you do not own in the belief that you can buy the share back at a lower price, thereby closing out the trade at a profit.

The mechanics of such a trade are as follows:

1 It is necessary to establish an equities account with your broker. This is not difficult, as anybody who has bought shares has such an account.

2 You inform your broker of the stock you wish to short-sell. Under the rules of the Australian Stock Exchange, there is a list of shares that your are permitted to short-sell. This list is shown in Appendix B.

3 Before you short-sell any shares, you will be required to lodge with your broker an initial margin of not less than 20% of the value of the contract price of the short-sale. This margin exists for both your protection and the broker's. Such a margin may be cash, or some other form of security such as shares.

4 Your short-sale must be disclosed to both the market and the exchange so as to maintain a fully-informed market.

5 Your broker may enter into an agreement to borrow scrip on your behalf to settle the transaction. It is important that you understand the way share settlement works in Australia. Your broker will be required to provide the counterpart to your transaction with the necessary paperwork to complete the transaction. This will mean they will have to borrow scrip from someone. Like any form of lending, this will incur a fee.

6 Should you get the trade wrong and the security you have short-sold rises, you will be required to lodge additional security with your broker to cover any additional margin calls.

7 When you buy the underlying security back, your margins are returned to you.

To examine how this works in practice, let's return to our example of Crown Casino. Let's assume that we have informed our broker of our intention to take advantage of short-selling opportunities, so all the necessary paperwork is up to speed.

In short-selling Crown Casino, we inform our broker of our desire to short-sell 10,000 shares at $2. Because the total value of such a transaction is $20,000, our initial margin of 20% is $4,000, which we lodge with the broker before the trade is initiated. It is important to note that in short-selling, there are rules pertaining to how an order can be placed. We cannot wade into the market and begin selling at market in the hope of driving the price down. According to the rules of the exchange, a short-sale must not be made at a price lower than the price at which the last reported sale of the security was made during the course of business for that day.

Our initial sale is at $2.00, and the reversal signal is given at $1.50, hence the initial profit on the trade is 50¢ per share, or $5,000.

A second short-sale signal is given at $1.55, and the reversal signal is given at $1.05, yielding a profit of 50¢ per share, or $5,000.

The total profit on this trade is $5,000 + $5,000 = $10,000, or 50% of the initial value of the short-sale. Costs such as brokerage and the fee for borrowing scrip have not been taken into consideration.

This outcome must be compared to the fate of those who sat and watched the gradual erosion of their equity. Whereas we have been able to generate a profit of $10,000 on a short-sale of $20,000, an investor who bought 10,000 Crown shares at $2 each and then failed to listen to what the market was telling them would have lost $10,000. Effectively, we have shifted $10,000 from the account of the ill-informed investor into our account.

The passive investor who took a long position in Crown at $2.00 when we were short-selling would, at the time of writing, have seen the value of their investment decay to 35¢, a loss of 82%. This remaining equity will have to grow 571% in a single year for this investor to return to their starting point, or, alternatively, at 100% per year for around 2.5 years (note that this is the rate of growth required to get the initial investment back, not to make any money). If you know of an investment that grows at a rate of 100% per year, I would certainly like to hear from you.

"Effectively, we have shifted $10,000 from the account of the ill-informed investor into our account."

Short-selling is a very under-utilised technique in Australia. Market participants tend to shy away from it due to ignorance, both on their behalf and their broker's. Successful short-selling is dependent upon having a methodology that can identify weakness in the price-action of a given stock.

9: PORTFOLIO MANAGEMENT USING DERIVATIVES

SO FAR, WE have seen that the portfolio bear has two alternative strategies when it comes to bear markets. The first is to sell the basket of shares that are being held and retire from the market – a prudent, conservative strategy that is unfortunately very under-utilised. It is often an impossible job to convince market participants that there are times when they should not own shares, such is the dogmatic superstition surrounding the stock market. The second technique we looked at was short-selling, a technique designed to take advantage of the prolonged downtrend that shares can enter. In this chapter we will look at the use of exchange-traded options and warrants as a means to prosper from bear markets.

WARRANT TRADING FOR BEARS

FIG. 9.1 – BHP SELL SIGNALS (1997)

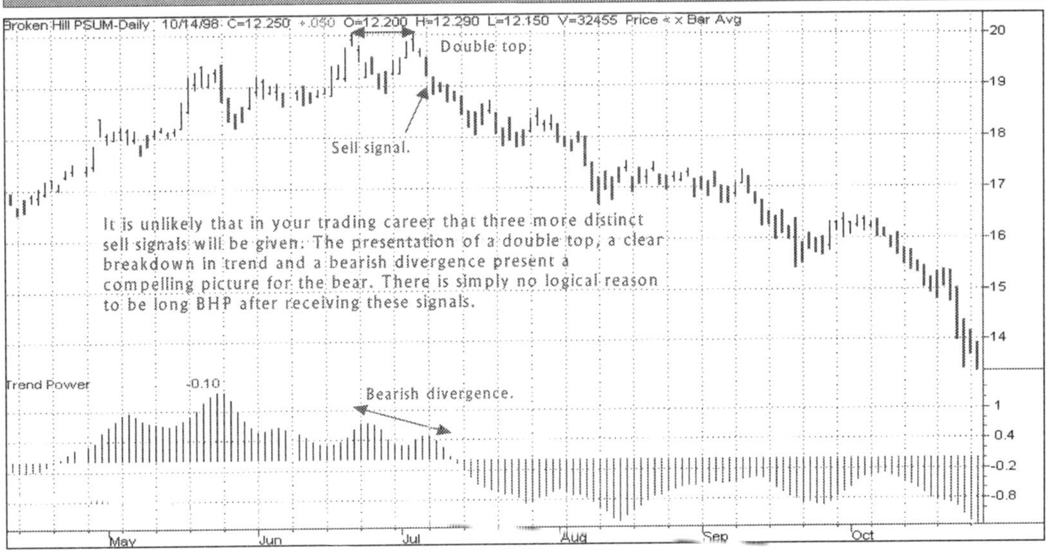

The chart on the previous page (Fig. 9.1) depicts BHP during its rather precipitous fall in the second half of 1997. Leading up to the fall, BHP had enjoyed a strong rally in concert with the rest of the market – then the wheels fell off. From a technical point of view, BHP gave a very strong sell signal with the presentation of a double top in late June. This is an extremely reliable technical indicator. The presence of a double top indicates a reluctance by traders to push prices beyond the previous high. It is a sign of weakness in price action, and is the harbinger of a decline in prices. The double top does not tell you how far prices will fall, but it does tell you they are weak and unstable. Further weight is given to the breakdown by the bearish divergence generated by the Trend Power oscillator.

"This chart was freely available to everyone. These are not secrets handed down like the ten commandments."

If you had seen this chart, there would be no conceivable reason why you would be a buyer of BHP. If you had been convinced by your broker, or some article you had read, that BHP was a good buy at $20, then you have a great deal of homework to do. You will never make any money listening to brokers or what you read in the financial press. This chart was freely available to everyone. These are not secrets handed down like the ten commandments. This information is available to anyone who takes the time to learn about it.

This breakdown in BHP presents us with an opportunity to profit from a bear market. Our tool for doing this is warrants.

Warrants come in a wide variety of types – we will not be going into the variety of sub-classes, these are more than adequately covered in material issued by ASX Derivatives. This section will solely concentrate on put warrants. Put warrants are essentially long-dated options that give the holder the right, but not the obligation, to sell the underlying share at a set price on or before a given expiry date. It is important to note that warrants can only be bought, they cannot be written.

In viewing our chart of BHP, and deciding that we wish to be short the stock, we are faced with our first decision: what warrant to buy? This decision is greatly simplified by the small number of put warrants available. Market participants are, by and large, bullish. This is evidenced by the fact that, irrespective of market conditions, there are always more bullish instruments traded than bearish. To draw on evidence from the exchange-traded options market, the number of call options traded always exceeds the number of put options traded, irrespective of whether the underlying stock is going up or down. The same situation applies to warrants. As BHP was falling, brokers were continually listing new call warrants, despite the fact that the price was sinking fast, and naïve traders were lapping them up.

In deciding which put warrant to buy, we follow virtually the same rules as were generated for selecting puts to trade the SPI. We base our decision on risk/reward criteria.

We know that the price is falling, but we do not know how far it will fall, so we stay as close to the money as possible in our selection. Remember, we want to profit from the fall, but we don't want to be left stranded with an out-of-the-money position should prices reverse.

In this case, our selection criteria guided us to the BHP 1700 March 98 put warrant (Fig. 9.2).

FIG. 9.2 – BHP PUT WARRANT BUY SIGNALS (1997)

As can be seen from the above chart (Fig. 9.2), this particular warrant demonstrated patterns that were the mirror-image of the underlying stock (Fig. 9.1). The price-action of this warrant generated buy signals that should have alerted the astute trader.

Since portfolio bears are, to a degree, interested in longer-term moves, it is necessary to look at the potential for a move to be sustained for a period of time. All traders should be aware that trends persist and should be followed. There are advantages and disadvantages to viewing data on a daily basis. The most obvious advantage is that it enables a very rapid response to any given signal. Signals are apparent at the end of a day's trading session. However, if followed too closely, daily signals may cause you to jump at shadows and leave a position pre-emptively, thereby missing a section of the move, or incurring additional transaction costs by having to re-enter a position after leaving it too early. You should stay with a trend until it ends, and often the only way to be sure that a trend has ended is to broaden the time-scale of your analysis.

The below chart (Fig. 9.3) is of our warrant on a weekly basis. All the indicators are now calculated on a weekly time frame, not a daily one.

FIG. 9.3 – BHP WEEKLY

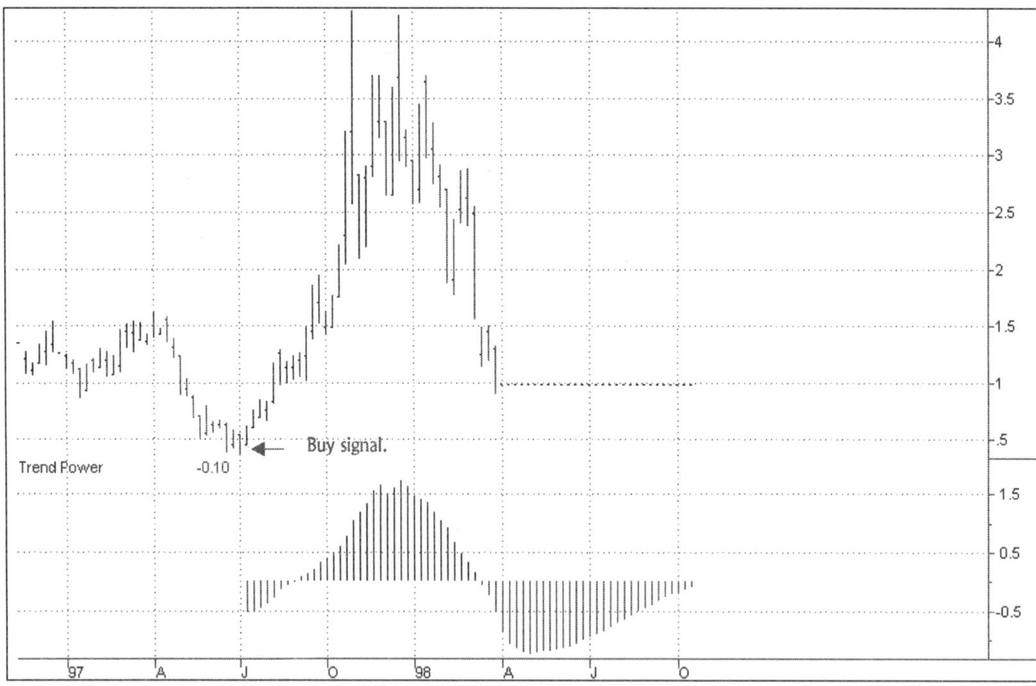

The advantage of viewing such a chart is that it keeps you in the trend for as long as possible. You will note that your entry point (55¢ to 60¢) into the trade is almost identical to that which could have been achieved using a daily chart. And, instead of perhaps whipsawing you out of the trend pre-emptively, it would have kept you in the trend until at least $3.

The successful trading of warrants is largely dependent upon the identification of the underlying trend. Many people approach the trading of derivatives as if it were a magic panacea. It is their belief that you can get the underlying direction of the trend wrong, but somehow still make money by using derivatives. Nothing could be further from the truth. All derivatives will enable you to do is to lose money more quickly if you get the direction wrong.

PORTFOLIO MANAGEMENT USING OPTIONS

> **"If the market is going down, you sell your portfolio and profit from the move down by trading."**

You will recall from the discussion of options on the SPI that a put option gives the holder the right, but not the obligation, to sell the underlying share at a set price by a set date. If we have an ANZ Dec 1100 put, we have the right, but not the obligation, to sell ANZ on or before the expiry date in December at $11. Portfolio bears seek to use put options for two purposes. First, to hedge their portfolios against any slippage in price. I do not believe in hedging. If the market is going down, you sell your portfolio and profit from the move down by trading. Hedging is not a trading tactic, it is an attempt to maintain the value of your shares in the face of a falling market. Despite misleading advertisements, hedging does not make you money, it merely preserves the status quo. In fact, hedging incurs a cost. Every time you hedge, you incur transaction costs. If the market is going down – *sell.*

The second reason people buy puts is to profit from any move down in share prices. This is how a bear trader should respond.

The below chart indicates a sell signal in the first week of May. Let's assume that we acted upon this signal and bought the August 1050 put for 35¢. Remember our selection criteria – we are trading to survive, so we use a more conservative strategy of buying an at-the-money option. Our strategy has a range of outcomes, shown on the following page.

FIG. 9.4 – NEWS CORP PUT OPTION BUYING (1997)

TABLE 9.1 – NEWS CORP PUTS

PRICE AT EXPIRY	OPTION PRICE	PROFIT/LOSS
1100	*0*	*-35*
1090	*0*	*-35*
1080	*0*	*-35*
1070	*0*	*-35*
1060	*0*	*-35*
1050	*0*	*-35*
1040	*10*	*-25*
1030	*20*	*-15*
1020	*30*	*-5*
1010	*40*	*5*
1000	*45*	*10*
990	*55*	*20*
980	*65*	*30*
970	*75*	*40*
960	*85*	*50*
950	*95*	*60*

NEWS CORP PUTS

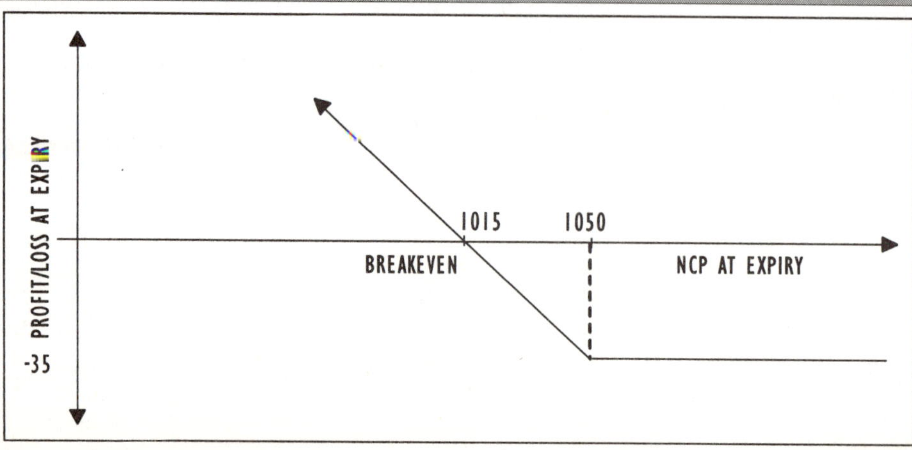

The profit from our trade is theoretically unlimited, and our loss is limited to our initial premium. We can never lose more than we paid for the option. This situation needs to be contrasted with the writing of call options as a bearish strategy. Assume that, upon viewing our chart of News Corp (Fig. 9.4), we decided to write the NCP August 1050 call for 45¢. The following outcomes are possible.

TABLE 9.2 – NEWS CORP CALLS

PRICE AT EXPIRY	OPTION PRICE	PROFIT/LOSS
1150	100	-55
1140	90	-45
1130	80	-35
1120	70	-25
1110	60	-15
1100	50	-5
1090	40	5
1080	30	15
1070	20	25
1060	10	35
1050	0	45
1040	0	45
1030	0	45
1020	0	45
1010	0	45
1000	0	45

NEWS CORP CALLS

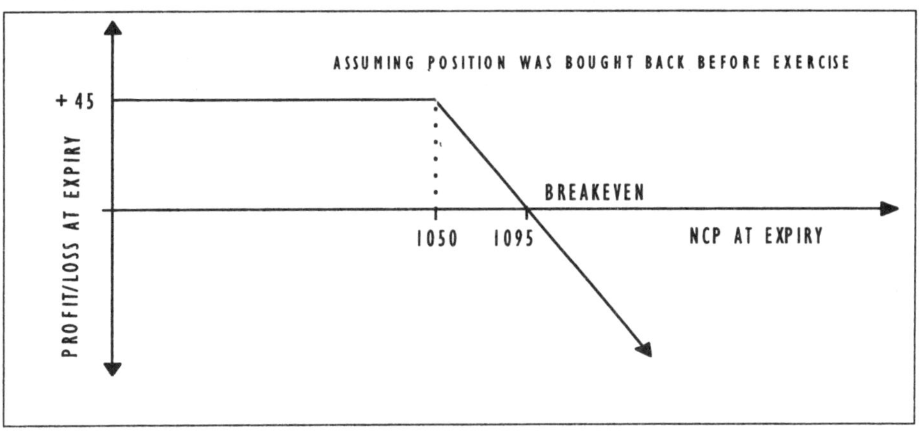

In selling calls, our profit is limited to the amount we received when we sold the calls, yet our potential loss is theoretically unlimited. In this example, for every cent NCP finishes above $10.95 in August, we are faced with a loss-making trade.

In this example, we have been slightly more aggressive than would be advisable. Our chances of surviving in options writing go up if we write out-of-the-money options. In this instance, it would have been more prudent to write the $11.00 call, to gain a wider margin of error.

RANGE TRADING

Range-trading stocks presents exactly the same challenge to bear traders as did range-trading the SPI. Once again, we need to look at specialist option strategies to take advantage of this drift in prices.

The Written Straddle

As can be seen from the chart below (Fig. 9.5), during June 1997 NAB shares traded between $18.50 and $19.00. Such price consolidation presents an opportunity to straddle the stock and take advantage of the inherent time decay.

FIG. 9.5 – NAB CONGESTION ZONE

To construct a written straddle, we sell options that have identical terms. For example, we would sell the NAB July 1850 call and put for 65¢ and 50¢ respectively. Such a strategy yields us $1.15 in premium income, hence we have a wide range over which the price of NAB can be at the time of expiry and still be profitable. Our upper boundary on the trade is $19.65 and the lower boundary is $17.35, so if NAB is inside this zone at the time of expiry the strategy will be profitable (shown below).

WRITTEN STRADDLE

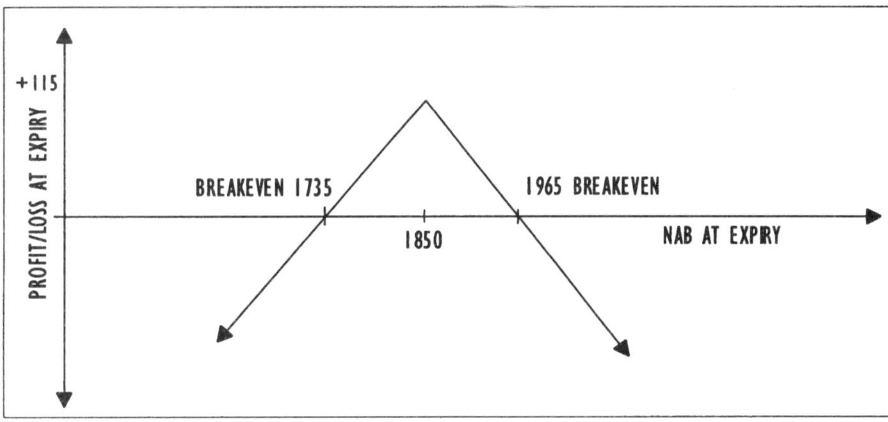

However, range-trading markets are very volatile and extremely dangerous for the unwary, due to the energy of the move that accompanies a break out of the trading range. Prices move very quickly once the trading range has been breached. This can be demonstrated if we look at the price history of NAB immediately after the break-out (Fig. 9.6).

FIG. 9.6 – NAB WRITTEN STRADDLE

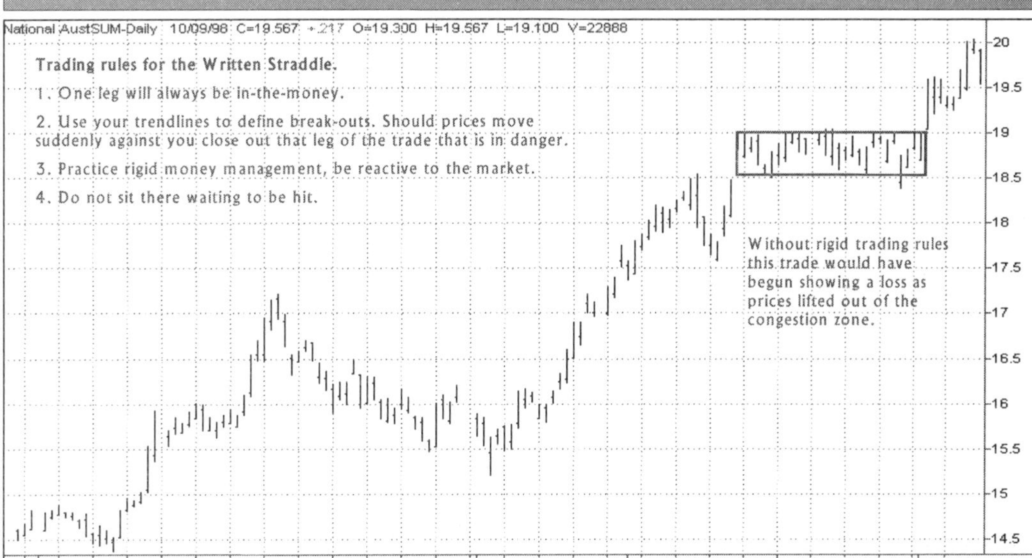

Before you attempt the written straddle, you must be absolutely confident in your ability to define a congestion zone, manage the risk inherent in this style of trade and thoroughly understand option dynamics.

"All prices eventually break out of consolidation – they often do this explosively. Such moves leave many traders flat-footed and faced with ever-increasing losses."

If you are uncertain of your ability to define what a congestion zone is then you need to review the stages of price evolution and the section on plotting trendlines, covered earlier in this book. Being able to set the upper and lower boundaries of price is essential to your survival. All prices eventually break out of consolidation – they often do this explosively. Such moves leave many traders flat-footed and faced with ever-increasing losses.

Since both legs of the written straddle are naked, you have to practise very tight money management. The liability involved in such a trade is high, and a fast moving market can bankrupt a trader.

Finally, you need to be cognisant of the dynamics of the options market. One leg of this trade is always in-the-money. It is possible that one leg of the trade may be exercised pre-emptively, i.e. before expiry. Such a development is uncommon, but it can happen. You cannot predict entirely the motivations of those who take the other side of a trade. Exercise is completely random, and once you have been exercised against there is nothing you can do about it.

The written straddle is a specialised, aggressive trading technique. You should not undertake it without fully understanding the risks involved, nor should you be seduced by the seemingly large amounts of premium income you can generate. This is the reward you receive for the high degree of risk you take on.

The Written Strangle

In our chart of Western Mining (WMC) on the opposite page (Fig 9.7), we can see that prices are trading in approximately a 50¢ band, between $5.00 and slightly-above $5.50. Such a wide, well-defined band enables bears to strangle the stock between two strike prices. In this instance, we would sell the WMC Sept 500 put for 20¢ and the WMC Sept 550 call for 25¢. Our strategy will be profitable if WMC continues to trade in this band until September. Our zone of profitability extends from $4.55 to $5.95, with our maximum profit being obtained if WMC finishes between the two strike prices at the end of September.

FIG. 9.7 – WMC WRITTEN STRANGLE

WRITTEN STRANGLE

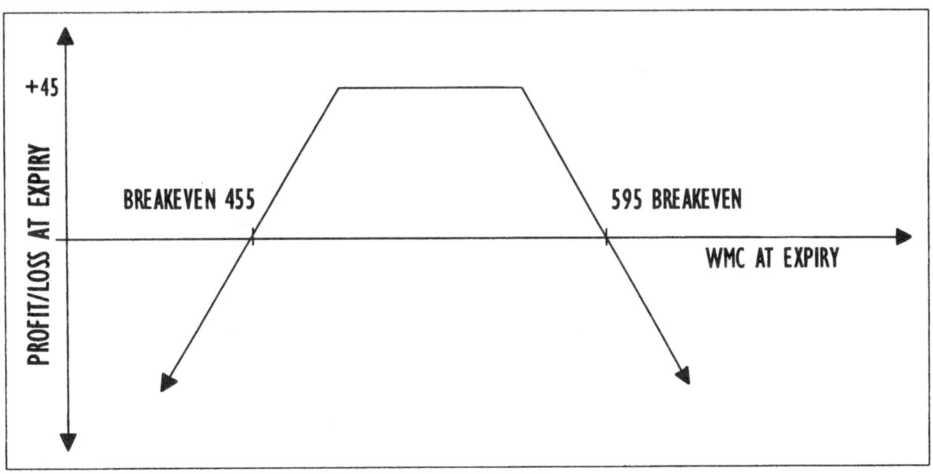

By definition, the written strangle is more conservative than the written straddle. However, there are still risks involved – you have naked option positions that offer you a limited profit potential for potentially unlimited loss. The major advantage of this strategy over the written straddle is that no leg of the trade is in-the-money unless the market moves sharply against you. There is also a wider zone of profitability, and this raises the chance of trader survival dramatically.

However, before you go generating written strangles everywhere, I want to reinforce what can happen when prices break out of congestion zones. In the WMC example, prices broke away from the zone of profitability under increasing volume – the bears were clearly in charge and pushing prices lower (Fig. 9.8). This was clearly the time to trade the prevailing trend. A written strategy in this situation is in trouble, and without quick follow-up action, will fail. You must return to the most basic of techniques – trading with the trend. However, if you cannot identify the trend then you will not be able to survive.

FIG. 9.8 – WMC DOWNWARD MOVEMENT

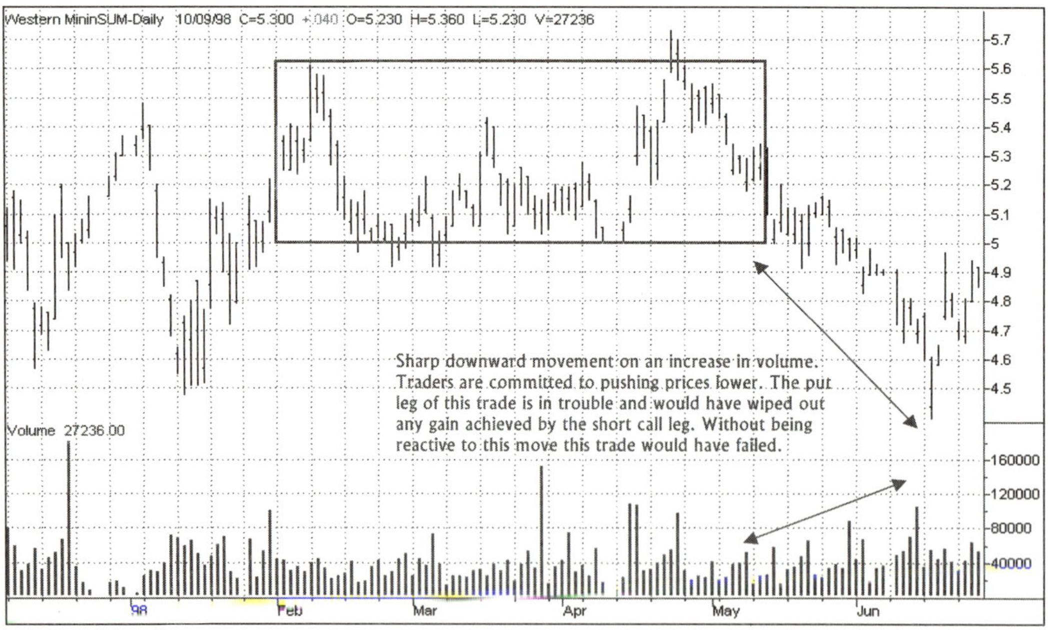

You must be a reactive trader and change with the prevailing market conditions. As was seen with WMC, the market swung from drifting to trending very quickly. You cannot predict this change, but you can equip yourself with an arsenal that can recognise it.

10: THE PERVERSITY OF MARKETS

THE CENTRAL IDEAS in this book have revolved around two key elements that are essential to success in trading any style of market. The first has been the need to develop your own methodology for engaging the market. The second is the need to separate yourself from the general mass who inhabit the market. Your opinions must be your own. You will not succeed in trading if you rely on others. If you still have not grasped this point, consider the following statistic: eight out of ten people who attempt to trade markets *fail*, completely and absolutely. Your chances of finding someone who has a better method than you are limited, so you might as well go with your own opinion.

However, the key point of this conclusion is not to labour the lack of success of others in the market. That is taken as fact. The key point is to demonstrate and reinforce both the seemingly perverse nature of the markets and the inability of the herd to understand their role in shaping the destiny of both the markets and themselves.

While I was writing this book, the world seemed to have gone on crash alert. Crash mania was gripping the financial world. The question I was most often asked was: when is the market going to crash? Not *if* the market was going to crash, but *when*. Now consider our bear market checklist. One of the key points of this checklist was: is everybody talking about the stock market and how wonderful it is? Just as we used this information as a guide to the general health of the market, we can use the reciprocal logic when it comes to thinking about bear markets and the potential for a sudden fall. If everybody is talking about the market crashing, then its chances of doing so diminish every day.

Eternal Bears

The crash maniacs seem to represent one particular psychological group: the eternal bears. This group – irrespective of market conditions – is always calling the top of the market. In their search for a rationale to back up their psychological profile, they have grasped for a variety of reasons as to why the market should suddenly plunge by 50%. These reasons include:

- A failure of the Dow to break through round numbers.
- Looming confrontation with Iraq.
- Looming confrontation with North Korea.
- Looming confrontation with Russia.
- The October effect – markets always crash in October is the general refrain.
- Elliott wave theory predicts a super-crash, when the Dow will fall to 100.
- General puritanical hysteria regarding Bill Clinton's inability to keep his pants up.
- World-wide doom and gloom – talk of a repeat of the depression of the 1930s.
- A sudden alignment of the planets (I am serious).
- The emergence of the millennium bug (now we are starting to get a little desperate).
- The failure of the National Basketball Association season in America to begin on time due to a dispute with players (I am not making this one up either).

Now compare this general bear paranoia with the opposite chart of the S&P500 (Fig. 10.1). Note what happened when dire warnings of the impending crash appeared on the front pages of four of America's most widely-read magazines. The market bounced, putting on 10% in value in seven days. In fact, this was the first time in a year that the US market had risen for seven consecutive days. If it is on the front page of a national magazine, then the chances of it happening are slim. Russell Sands – one of the original group of Turtle Traders (see *Market Wizards* by Jack Schwager) – said that the only system he ever bought that made him any money was one that tracked daily newspaper stories and then did exactly the opposite of what was either forecast or recommended. Remember, eight out of ten traders are losers. Simple number theory says that if you do the opposite to the losers then you have a chance of being a trader who makes money.

FIG. 10.1 – S&P500 MOVEMENT (1997)

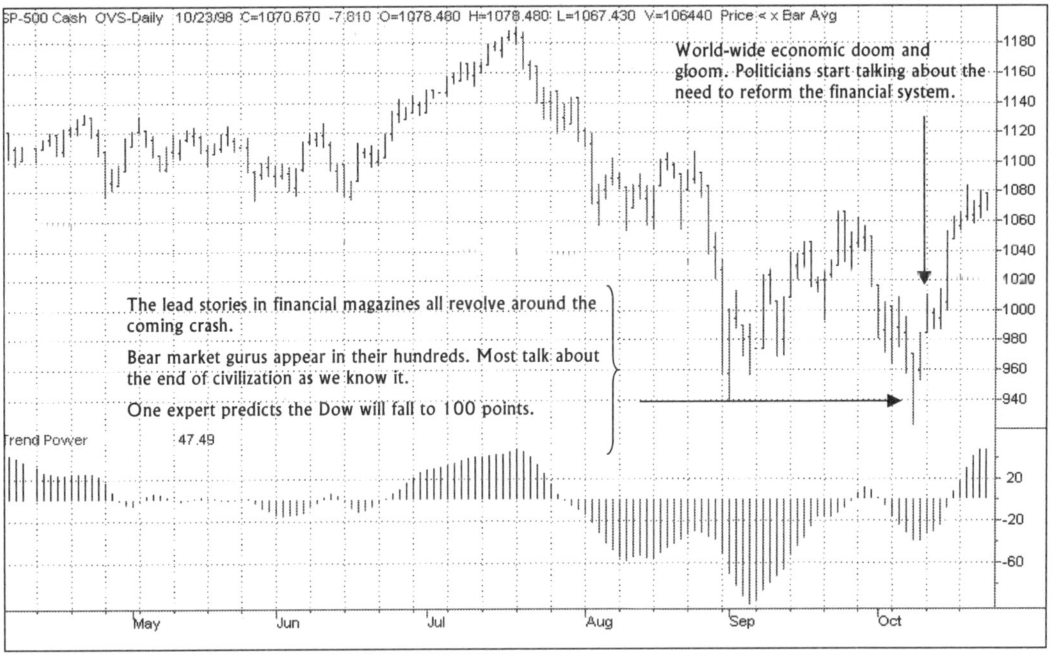

As a means of reinforcing the inability of experts – and I use the term loosely – to get it right, consider the chart of the All Ordinaries Index on the following page (Fig. 10.2). In the July edition of one leading investment magazine the lead story would have made you hide under your bed. The deadline for stories for these magazines is about four weeks prior to them hitting the newsagents, so this magazine made their call of catastrophe at the bottom of the swing down from the peak in mid-April. The market then reversed and put on almost 12%. If you had listened to this story, you would have missed out on this long-sided trade, thereby incurring an opportunity cost. You would also most likely have been facing in the wrong direction and incurred an actual trading loss by being short the market at its low point.

"As a means of reinforcing the inability of experts...to get it right, consider the following chart of the All Ordinaries Index."

The final point I will make – and it is one that has been illustrated by these examples of the S&P500 and the All Ordinaries Index – is that there really are no such things as bear market traders. There are traders who are continually bearish the market irrespective of the actual market conditions. Such traders do a lot of talking and a lot of searching for a rationale behind their negative outlooks, but they make very little money. Strangely enough, eternal bulls have the same problem.

FIG. 10.2 – ALL ORDINARIES MOVEMENT (1997)

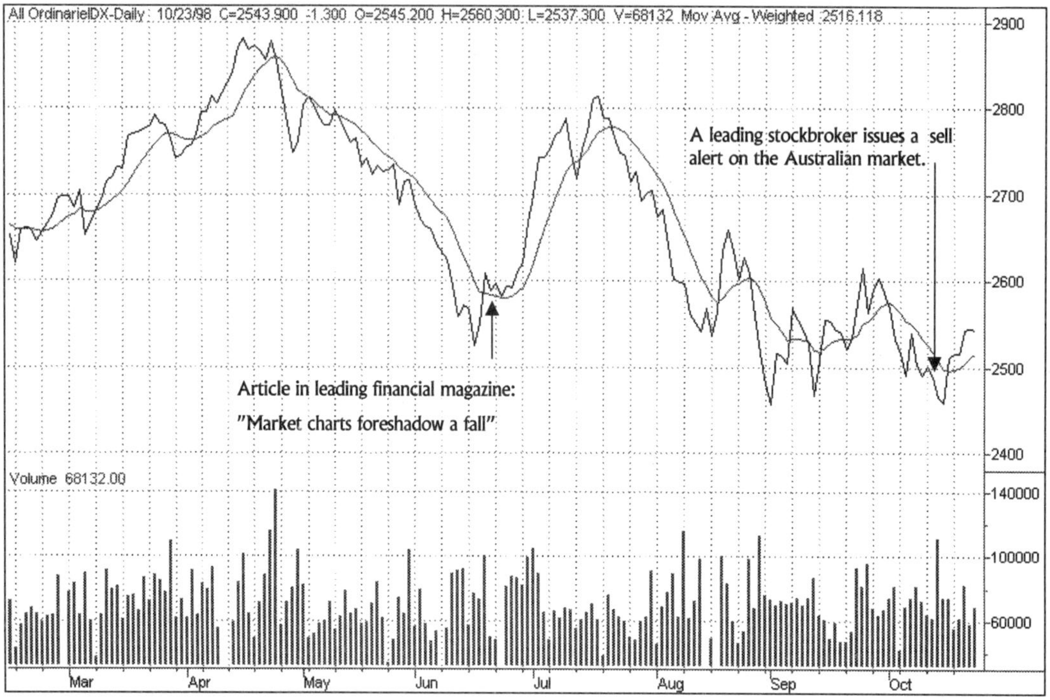

And so we return to the central themes of this book: the need for intellectual independence and a firm trading methodology. In the end, there are only traders with the mental flexibility to flow with market conditions. It is a somewhat hackneyed old phrase, but storms always blow oak trees over whilst willow trees somehow manage to survive. Trading is about surviving, and survival only comes from flexibility.

11: THE BEAR MARKET TRADER'S SURVIVAL GUIDE

THE FOLLOWING POINTS form a guide for the bear market trader. In fact, they are points that should be seared into the brain of any trader. If you are considering trading, or you are already a trader, these are some issues you should consider:

1. Be absolutely certain that you want to be a trader

Markets have been traded for several thousand years, and definitive records have been kept for in excess of 150 years. During this time, the rate of failure among speculators (i.e. traders) has remained constant at approximately eight out of ten. In the past 150 years, we have introduced new financial products, markets have been globalised and the computer has brought the stock market into every home. Despite this, the majority of people who trade fail dismally. However, this is not a negative message because it means that some people out there know what they are doing, and they are making all the money.

2. Examine your motives

One of the things that sets highly successful traders apart from the losers that make up the bulk of the trading community is that they understand their motives for trading. They know why they are traders, and surprisingly enough they are not traders to make money – the money is merely a side effect of trading well. If you are able to trade bear markets cleanly and precisely, the money will flow as a natural consequence of your skill.

Every trader should have listed the reasons why they want to trade, and this should form part of their trader's business plan. I very rarely use the word guaranteed in conjunction with trading, but if your prime motive for trading is to make money, then you are guaranteed to fail.

3. You must have a method

Throughout this book we have looked at a variety of techniques for trading markets. There are no shortage of indicators available. Most are serviceable, and will assist you in your trade selection. Irrespective of the method you use, your system must follow a few basic rules:

- *It must be trend-following.* You will never make any money if you do not understand that the trend is boss. Trying to counter-trend trade simply does not work.
- *It must be robust.* Market conditions change over time. As we have seen, markets can move from trending to congesting very quickly. Your method must be able to identify these changes in market tone.
- *The simpler your method the better.* This is the reason I developed a largely mechanical system for my own use. It removes me and my personality from the decision-making process.
- *Forget trying to predict the future.* Both you and your system should be reactive. Your predictions as to where the market may or may not go are simply irrelevant. You should forget all about Gann, Elliott Wave, astrology and all the other nonsense that permeates the financial markets.
- *Your method must be testable.* Traders by and large do not understand the difference between correlation and coincidence. For example, if a magazine article tells me something is going up and it does, I know from experience that this is coincidence. However, if my system tells me that the All Ordinaries Index is going down and it does, I know this to be a result of correlation.
- *The approach you take to the market should include strict rules for trade entry and exit.* And remember, these are useless if you do not stick to them.

4. You must have an edge

Your method gives you an edge. If you do not know what your edge is then you are guaranteed to fail.

5. Developing an effective method is hard work

To successfully engage any market with an adequate methodology takes time and hard work. Expect set-backs.

6. *Hard work versus skill*

You can only get so far with hard work. It is possible to improve your trading, probably beyond any point you thought possible. Sooner or later, though, you will plateau. This is simply the way the world operates. Some people will go further than others simply because of innate skill.

7. *Trading should be effortless*

If your trading causes you pain or unsettles you emotionally, you are not equipped to be a trader. As an example, consider this simple test: does your trading keep you awake at night? If it does, you should withdraw from the market permanently because you lack the required emotional and psychological skills to be a trader. This is nothing to be ashamed of – all of us have endeavours that we simply cannot do. It is essential to realise that not everybody can be a trader. Acceptance of this is vital to your emotional and financial well being.

8. *Money management and risk control*

Etch this rule into your brain. TRADE TO SURVIVE, TRADE TO SURVIVE, TRADE TO SURVIVE. This rule should permeate everything you do in the markets. If you adopt this approach, you will be around long enough to make money. You must keep your position size as small as possible to minimise your risk of a catastrophic loss. Remember, if you lose 50% of your equity then you will have to make 100% to merely break even.

9. *The trading plan*

My rule for this is simple: proper prior preparation prevents poor performance. All trades must be planned in advance. This plan must include what your money management criteria are, how much you are going to risk on the trade, what your reasons are for entering the trade, what you are going to do once you are in the trade and what conditions will cause you to exit the trade. Your plan should also have follow-up action should you make either a loss or a profit.

10. *Discipline*

No discipline, no profit. It is that simple. Trading choppy markets is not something you make up as you go along. You must stick to your trading plan – no deviation should be tolerated.

11. Understand that you are responsible

Everything that happens to you in the market is your fault. Traders tend to abrogate responsibility for their mistakes to a perceived higher authority. The excuses as to why people lose money are many and varied, and include statements such as "my broker cost me money" or "only insiders make money". The common theme is a lack of personal responsibility. This is particularly prevalent among traders who cannot trade bear markets. In the case of a bear market, all you need say is that you didn't make any money – or you lost money – because the market is going down. The market is to blame for your failure. However, the market does not force you to participate. It does not force you to hold losing positions or attempt to buy in a falling market. These are your decisions. If you cannot come to grips with this most essential of features, you are not equipped to be a trader.

12. Be independent

In a summary of adviser expectations for the period 1965 to 1988 (similar to that done for mutual funds, as seen in Chapter 1), expectations were divided into either bullish or bearish for the year ahead. These expectations were then reviewed to ascertain their veracity. In the 23-year sample period, the financial community were right on only three occasions. These can be put down to coincidence.

13. Losing is part of the game

All traders will lose money at some stage in their career. It is inevitable. One of the key psychological features that separates successful traders from unsuccessful traders is their capacity to deal with losses. Winning traders accept that they will have losses, but these will not affect their long-term prospects. Losing traders operate under a completely different mindset. They assume that they must never lose money – ever. This results in an inability to accept small losses. Eventually these small losses become catastrophic losses that bring a rapid end to their careers as traders. Poor traders cannot see past their losses and envisage profitable trades in the future. They believe that one loss will be followed by another in a never-ending continuum. If they have no trading system and no discipline then this is probably what will happen. However, if they do have a tested methodology and are disciplined in its application, then they will have to accept that no method is perfect and they will get bad trades, but this does not instantly invalidate their method.

Paradoxically, successful traders believe that a trade where they have followed their rules and made a loss is a successful trade. They know that if they can follow their rules through a poor trade then they can follow them through good trades.

14. The virtue of patience

Throughout this book I have tried to stress that the market will always tell you what to do. There are actually very few surprises in trading, and this applies to holding positions. Too often traders set themselves narrow profit targets and then leap off the trade the moment these targets have been reached. Such traders then exclude themselves from the rest of the move. I have seen many traders take 50 points of a 300 point move merely because that is the arbitrary profit target they have set themselves. If you have a trend-following method, combined with strong money management, then the market will tell you when to exit a trade. Trends exist to be followed. Predicting how far a trend will take you in advance is rather like a surfer trying to predict how far a wave they are yet to catch will take them.

15. Learn to be disloyal

The position is not your friend. It does not even know you exist. When the market tells you to leave, leave.

16. Being right is more important than being a genius

As traders, we are only seeking to catch the major part of a trend – the top and the bottom are irrelevant. These are the preserve of traders who want to be heroes, and there are no successful hero traders, only profitable survivors.

17. Hope is a four letter word

There is no such thing as hope in trading, nor does the power of prayer seem to hold much sway with the market. If a trade has gone wrong it has gone wrong – all the best will in the world will not alter this fact. If it has gone wrong, exit the position immediately.

18. You cannot win if you have to

Do not play with money you cannot afford to lose. If you are becoming a trader in some desperate last stand to avoid financial disaster then your failure is guaranteed. Only trade with money you can afford to lose. There is a simple reason for this – you will be more relaxed and you will be able to take losses when they occur. Trading with money you cannot afford to lose brings with it enormous stress, and this in turn magnifies the chance of making an error that will be catastrophic.

19. The markets are an expensive place to look for excitement

It has been my experience that trading is a fairly routine, boring activity. You analyse the markets in the same way using the same tools every day. There is very little variety. The popular image of trading is a group of individuals standing around yelling and wildly gesticulating about the price of pork bellies. This is not the world of trading. Trading is calm, dispassionate, disciplined and at times very isolated. If you wish to throw money around in a search for excitement, visit Crown Casino. They could do with the help.

20. Prices are not random

This is an old chest-nut usually trotted out by fund managers when they are asked why – when they are paid $500,000 a year – they cannot beat the All Ordinaries Index. The common response is that the markets are random. Such an idea was discredited long ago. You can, if you are willing to learn and apply yourself, beat the market.

NCP DIVERGENCES

The above chart shows the divergences on the NCP chart on page 60.

APPENDIX B: APPROVED COMPANIES FOR SHORT-SELLING

ABF ABERFOYLE LTD
AAA ACACIA RESOURCES LTD
ADB ADELAIDE BANK LTD
ABC ADELAIDE BRIGHTON CEMENT HOLDINGS LTD
APF ADVANCE PROPERTY FUND
AMC AMCOR LTD
AOF AMP OFFICE TRUST
AML AMRAD CORPORATION LTD
ANL ANACONDA NICKEL NL
ARG ARGO INVEMENTS LTD
ALL ARISTOCRAT LEISURE LTD
AJO ARMSTRONG JONES OFFICE FUND
AJR ARMSTRONG JONES RETAIL FUND
ASH ASHTON MINING LTD
APY ASIA PACIFIC SPECIALTY CHEMICALS LTD
AUG AURORA GOLD LTD
AUD AUSDOC GROUP LTD
ASL AUSDRILL LIMITED
ANE AUSPINE LTD
ANZ AUSTRALIA AND NEW ZEALAND BANKING GROUP LTD
AFI AUSTRALIAN FOUNDATION INVESTMENT COMPANY LTD
AGL AUSTRALIAN GAS LIGHT COMPANY (THE)
AHX AUSTRALIAN HEALTH CARE LTD
AIX AUSTRALIAN INFRASTRUCTURE GROUP
ANI AUSTRALIAN NATIONAL INDUSTRIES LTD
APN AUSTRALIAN PROVINCIAL NEWSPAPERS HOLDINGS LTD
ARS AUSTRALIAN RESOURCES LTD
ATU AUSTRALIAN TOURISM GROUP
ARL AUSTRIM LTD
AWA AWA LTD
AZO AZON LTD
BAA BAA PLC
BQD BANK OF QUEENSLAND LTD
BWA BANK OF WESTERN AUSTRALIA LTD
BMT BARCLAYS - MIRVAC PROPERTY TRUST
BTA BIOTA HOLDINGS LTD
BOR BORAL LTD
BOC BOUGANVILLE COPPER LTD
BIL BRAMBLES INDUSTRIES LTD
BRY BRIERLEY INVESTMENTS LTD
BRL BRL HARDY LTD
BBP BROKEN HILL PROPRIETARY CO. LTD (THE)
BTE BT AUSTRALIAN EQUITY MANAGEMENT LTD
BHT BT HOTEL GROUP
BTP BT PROPERTY TRUST
BTL BTR PLC
BPC BURNS, PHILP AND COMPANY LTD
BIR BURSWOOD LTD
CTX CALTEX AUSTRALIA LTD
CPY CAPCOUNT PROPERTY TRUST
CPL CAPITAL PROPERTY TRUST
CAA CAPRAL ALUMINIUM LTD
CHY CARTER HOLT HARVEY LTD
CTR CENTAUR MINING AND EXPLORATION LTD
CEQ CENTRAL EQUITY LIMITED
CEP CENTRO PROPERTIES GROUP
CIH CHINA CONSTRUCTION HOLDINGS LTD
CIM CIM RESOURCES LTD
CMX CLIMAX MINING LTD
COA COATES HIRE LIMITED
CCL COCA-COLA AMATIL LTD
COH COCHLEAR LTD
CML COLES MYER LTD
COT COLLY COTTON LIMITED
COC COLONIAL COMMERCIAL PROPERTY TRUST
CIP COLONIAL INDUSTRIAL PROPERTY TRUST
CGH COLONIAL LIMITED
CMF COLONIAL MUTUAL AUSTRALIAN PROPERTY FUND
CMC COMALCO LTD
CBA COMMONWEALTH BANK OF AUSTRALIA
CMG COMMONWEALTH INSTALMENT RECEIPT TRUSTEE LTD
CRT CONSOLIDATE RUTILE LTD
CWI COUNTRY WIDE RETAIL TRUST
CRO CROWN CASINO LTD
CSD CRUSADER LTD
CSL CSL LTD
CSR CSR LTD
CLR CULTUS PETROLEUM NL
DJS DAVID JONES LTD
DVD DAVIDS LTD
DGD DELTA GOLD NL
DJW DJERRIWARRH INVESTMENTS LTD
EMN EAGLE MINING CORPORATION NL
EAM EASTERN ALUMINIUM LTD
EAL ELDERS AUSTRALIA LTD

ELT	ELTIN LTD
EML	EMAIL LTD
EMP	EMPEROR MINES LTD
ENE	ENERGY DEVELOPMENTS LIMITED
EEC	ENERGY EQUITY CORPORATION LTD
ERA	ENERGY RESOURCES OF AUSTRALIA LTD
ERG	E.R.G. AUSTRALIA LTD
EDI	EVANS DEAKIN INDUSTRIES LTD
ENV	ENVESTRA LTD
FAI	FAI INSURANCE LTD
FXJ	FAIRFAX (JOHN HOLDINGS LTD)
FHF	FAULDING (F.H. & CO LTD)
FAF	FIVE ARROWS AUSTRALIA LTD (THE)
FLC	FLETCHER CHALLENGE LTD
FOA	FOODLAND ASSOCIATED LTD
FBG	FOSTER'S BREWING GROUP LTD
FIF	FRANKED INCOME FUND (THE)
FCL	FUTURIS CORPORATION LTD
GAN	GANDEL RETAIL TRUST
GPT	GENERAL PROPERTY TRUST
GIO	GIO AUSTRALIA HOLDINGS LTD
GLD	GOLDFIELDS LTD
GKL	GOLDFIELDS KALGOORLIE LTD
GMF	GOODMAN FIELDER WATTIE LTD
GST	GPT SPLIT TRUST
GCM	GREAT CENTRAL MINES NL
GUD	G.U.D. HOLDINGS LTD
GSP	GUINNESS PEAT GROUP PLC
GWT	GWA INTERNATIONAL LTD
HVN	HARVEY NORMAN LTD
HIH	HEATH (CE INTERNATIONAL HOLDINGS LTD)
HPT	HEINE INDUSTRIAL PROPERTY TRUST
HRW	HENRY WALKER GROUP LTD
HIL	HILLS INDUSTRIES LIMITED
HLY	HILLS MOTORWAY GROUP
HLN	HOLYMAN LTD
HOY	HOYTS CINEMAS GROUP
IAM	I.A.M.A. LTD
ICT	INCITEC LTD
IFT	INFRASTRUCTURE TRUST OF AUSTRALIA GROUP
HAH	JAMES HARDIE INDUSTRIES LTD
JUP	JUPITERS LTD
JJS	JUST JEANS GROUP LTD
LAC	LANG CORPORATION LTD
LEI	LEIGHTON HOLDINGS LTD
LLC	LEND LEASE CORPORATION LTD
LHG	LIHIR GOLD LTD
LNN	LION NATIONAL LTD
MAH	MACMAHON HOLDINGS LTD
MBL	MACQUARIE BANK LTD
MMC	MACRAES MINING COMPANY LTD
MAY	MAYNE NICKLESS LTD
MTL	METALCORP LIMITED
MMF	METAL MANUFACTURES LTD
MWB	METWAY BANK LTD
MIM	M.I.M. HOLDINGS LTD
MRV	MIRVAC LTD
MMU	MMI LTD
MBC	MOBILE COMMUNICATIONS HOLDINGS LTD
MLG	MT LEYSON GOLD MINES LTD
NAB	NATIONAL AUSTRALIA BANK LTD
NCL	NATIONAL CONSOLIDATED LTD
NFD	NATIONAL FOODS LTD
NPT	NATIONAL INDUSTRIAL PROPERTY TRUST
NMH	NATIONAL MUTUAL HOLDINGS LTD
NMP	NATIONAL MUTUAL PROPERTY TRUST
NCM	NEWCREST MINING LTD
NCP	NEWS CORPORATION LTD (THE)
NML	NIUGINI MINING LTD
NDY	NORMANDY MINING LTD
NBH	NORTH LTD
NFM	NORTH FLINDERS MINES LTD
NVS	NOVUS PETROLEUM LTD
OSH	OIL SEARCH LTD
OPS	OPSM PROTECTOR LTD
OEC	ORBITAL ENGINE CORPORATION LTD
ORI	ORICA LTD
OML	OROGEN MINERALS LTD
PDP	PACIFIC DUNLOP LTD
PLS	PAULS LTD
PBB	PACIFICA GROUP LTD
PDC	PALADIN COMMERCIAL TRUST
PMP	PMP COMMUNICATION LTD
PAS	PASMINCO LTD
PTZ	PETROZ NL
PSA	PETSEC ENERGY LTD
PNI	PIONEER INTERNATIONAL LTD
PLP	PLACER PACIFIC LTD
PLU	PLUTONIC RESOURCES LTD
PMM	PORTMAN MINING LIMITED
PRP	PRIME CREDIT PROPERTY TRUST
PIP	PRIME INDUSTRIAL PROPERTY TRUST
PRT	PRIME TELEVISION LIMITED
PII	PROPERTY INCOME INVESTMENT TRUST
PBL	PUBLISHING & BROADCASTING LTD
QAN	QANTAS AIRWAYS LTD
QBE	QBE INSURANCE GROUP LTD

QRL QCT RESOURCES LIMITED
QNI QNI LTD
QMC QUEENSLAND METALS CORPORATION LTD
RAC REINSURANCE AUSTRALIA CORP. LTD
RSG RESOLUTE SAMANTHA LTD
RGC RGC LTD
RIC RIDLEY CORPORATION LTD
RSM ROSS MINING NL
RTH ROTHMANS HOLDINGS LTD
RUP RURAL PRESS LTD
STO SANTOS LTD
SVR SAVAGE RESOURCES LTD
SCR SCHRODERS INT'L PROPERTY FUND NV
SCH SCHRODERS PROPERTY FUND
SWD SEA WORLD PROPERTY TRUST
SEV SEVEN NETWORK LTD
SGI SGIO INSURANCE LTD
SID SIDDONS RAMSET LTD
SMS SIMSMETAL LTD
SKE SKILLED ENGINEERING LTD
SMI SMITH (HOWARD LTD)
SHL SONIC HEALTHCARE LIMITED
SGW SONS OF GWALIA LTD
SRP SOUTHCORP HOLDINGS LTD
SPP SOUTHERN PACIFIC PETROLEUM NL
SCP SPICERS PAPER LTD
SPT SPOTLESS GROUP LTD
SPS SPOTLESS SERVICES LTD
SBM ST BARBARA MINES LTD
SGB ST GEORGE BANK LTD
SGP STOCKLAND TRUST GROUP
SYD SYDNEY HARBOUR CASINOS HOLDINGS LTD
TAH TABCORP HOLDINGS LTD
TAP TAP OIL NL
TEL TELECOM CORPORATION OF NZ LTD
TMS TELEVISION & MEDIA SERV. DAVIDS LTD
TOR TICOR LTD
TLSCA TELSTRA CORPORATION LTD
THG THAKRAL HOLDINGS GROUP
TLA TOURISM AND ASSET HOLDINGS LIMITED
TYA TYNDALL AUSTRALIA LTD
VRL VILLAGE ROADSHOW LTD
WKC WALKER CORPORATION LTD
WYL WATTYL LTD
WHW WD & HO WILLS HOLDINGS LTD
WES WESFARMERS LTD
WAN WEST AUSTRALIAN NEWSPAPERS HOLDINGS LTD
WMT WESTERN METALS LTD
WMC WESTERN MINING CORP. HOLDINGS LTD
WFA WESTFIELD AMERICA TRUST
WSF WESTFIELD HOLDINGS LTD
WFT WESTFIELD TRUST
WBC WESTPAC BANKING CORPORATION LTD
WPT WESTPAC PROPERTY TRUST
WSL WESTRALIAN SANDS LTD
WPL WOODSIDE PETROLEUM LTD
WOW WOOLWORTHS LTD

NOTE

The companies on this list have:

(i) a market capitalisation of at least $100 million;

(ii) at least 50 million units on issue, excluding holdings by a related entity; and

(iii) Australia as the major market for their securities.

** Any company under takeover is unable to be short-sold*

GLOSSARY

American option An American-style option allows the option holder to exercise the option any time during the life of the contract up to and including the day of expiry.

At-the-market An order to buy or sell at the prevailing market price irrespective of price level. A quick and easy way to get in or out of the market; although don't be surprised if in a fast moving market your order is not filled at the price you expected.

At-the-money An option is said to be at-the-money when its exercise price is equal to the current market price of the underlying futures contract. For example, a March 2500 SPI option will be at-the-money if the SPI is trading at 2500.

Average down In my opinion, to buy more of a security the price of which has declined is a recipe for disaster. This is akin to hanging onto the deck of the Titanic as it went down.

Bear/Bearish A bear is someone with a negative expectation of the market. The true origin of the expression is unclear. Traditionally it is thought that bears claw back market gains.

Beta A measure of volatility in share and futures trading. Beta measures the movement of a given instrument relative to a benchmark such as a composite index. By definition the All Ordinaries Index has a beta of 1.0, if a stock has a beta of less than 1.0 then its price will rise or fall proportionally less than the overall market.

Breakeven point The price at which a trade neither makes nor loses money.

Bull/Bullish Someone who expects prices to rise.

Buying hedge A hedge against an increase in the cost of a commodity.

Call option A call option gives the holder the right, but not the obligation, to buy the underlying commodity at given price up to and including the day of expiry.

Close out The process of taking the opposite side of a transaction in order to liquidate or nullify the position. If I had a bought futures contract I would close it out by selling it.

Closing sale Any trade that liquidates a trader's bought position. For example, if I had BHP 1800 puts and I sold them then this would be a closing sale.

Day only order An order that remains open until the close of business.

Day trading Buying and selling within a single trading session. In general, it can be a most unprofitable venture.

Default A bad thing and something that, to my knowledge, is quite rare. It is the failure to honour your obligations under the terms of either the specifications of the contract – such as a failure to take delivery – or the failure to meet a margin call.

Deliverable types Any physical commodity that can be delivered, e.g. wool.

Deposit Also known as the *initial margin*, it is the amount of money a broker will ask you for before you open a position and then, depending on how your trade is going, periodically throughout the life of the trade.

Discount An option is said to be trading at a discount when it is trading for less than its intrinsic value.

Discretionary account Not something you are likely to encounter. It is an account where the broker is able to make trades on a client's account without reference to the client. You should never give responsibility for your trades to anyone else.

Downside protection Insurance against any downward move in the underlying stock. Buying puts against physical stock or buying and writing confer downside protection.

Early exercise Not something a naked option writer looks forward to. Early exercise refers to any option that is exercised prior to the expiry date.

Endowment warrant A warrant where the outstanding balance is paid for by the accumulation of dividends from the underlying share.

European option An option contract that only allows exercise on the date of expiry.

Exchange-traded option See *American option*. An option to take up an underlying futures position.

Exercise To invoke the right that is attached to an option contract. For example, if I own a call option I have the right to buy the underlying stock at a given price. If I choose to take up the underlying stock I have exercised my right under the terms of the contract.

Exercise price Also known as the *strike price*, this is the price at which an option may be exercised.

Hedge A mechanism whereby a futures position is taken so as to minimise any adverse price movements in the physical market.

Historical volatility A measure of how much the price of a commodity has moved over a given period of time.

In-the-money When the exercise price of a call (put) is below (above) the current market value of the underlying contract.

Intrinsic value In-the-money options are said to possess intrinsic value. This is defined as the difference in price between the exercise price of the option and the price of the underlying contract. For example, if a 2550 SPI option was trading at 50 points and the SPI was trading at 2540, then this option would have 40 points of intrinsic value and 10 points of time value.

Legging it in A mechanism whereby trades involving many variables, such as in complex spreads, are done one leg at a time rather than simultaneously.

Liquidation To unwind an existing position. A long position is liquidated by taking an offsetting short position and a short position is liquidated by taking an offsetting long position.

Liquid market A market with a great deal of activity. The SPI is a liquid market; share futures are not.

Long Any trader who has a bought futures contract is said to be long.

Margin An additional deposit required from a client when a futures contract moves against them. If the position were to be closed out immediately prior to margin call it would show a loss.

Margin call The dreaded phone call from the broker who says: "We need more money – you have got it wrong." Successful traders cut losing positions as soon as it becomes apparent that something has gone wrong. Poor traders do not.

Market order An order to buy at market irrespective of the prevailing price.

Naked option A position where the writer of an option does not own the underlying security. By definition all written puts are naked.

Neutral A situation where you expect the market to remain fairly constant. You are neither bullish nor bearish. An example of a neutral strategy would be a written straddle.

Out-of-the-money A call option with a strike price higher or a put option with a strike price lower than the underlying contract is said to be out-of-the-money.

Overbought Relative term used to describe the perception that prices have been pushed up to what is thought to be an unsustainable high level.

Oversold The opposite of *overbought.*

Payoff diagrams The funny little charts in the latter half of this book. Typically they are used to give a visual interpretation of the range of outcomes for various strategies.

Premium A catch-all term generally used to describe the difference in value of one futures contract over another.

Price-to-earnings ratio Calculated by dividing the current market price by earnings.

Profit range The prime consideration for any trader. It is the range of prices within which an options strategy will make a profit.

Put option The option to take a sold futures contract at a predetermined price.

Rally An upward move in price.

Selling hedge A technique by which futures are sold to hedge against a perceived possibility of a decline in price.

Short A sold futures position. A holder of put options is said to be short the market.

Short-selling The strategy of selling an instrument that you do not already own in the belief that the price will fall and the security can be bought back at a lower price. For example, if I were to short-sell BHP at $19.00 my belief would be that I could buy it back at below $19.00.

Speculator A trader who is only interested in trading changes in price. On the whole, a fairly unsuccessful group. It is often said that in futures markets 10% of the people make 90% of the money.

Straddle In futures parlance, the purchase of one month against the sale of another month. Such a trade is based upon the belief that the price relationship or spread between the two contracts will change. Also referred to as an options trade where options with the same terms are either bought or sold.

Strangle A strategy that requires the buying or writing of two options, a put and a call. The strategy requires that the options used must be of the same expiry date but with different strike prices. The object of a strangle is to squeeze a stock between two strike prices.

Switch Rolling from one contract to another. Involves closing one position and simultaneously opening another in the same commodity.

Trend The thing you want to be on – the general direction of the market.

Volatility The degree to which the price of an underlying security could reasonably be expected to move.

Warrant An option that has been issued by a third party and is traded on the ASX.

Writer The seller of an option.

INDEX

P

Q

R

S

T